I0095663

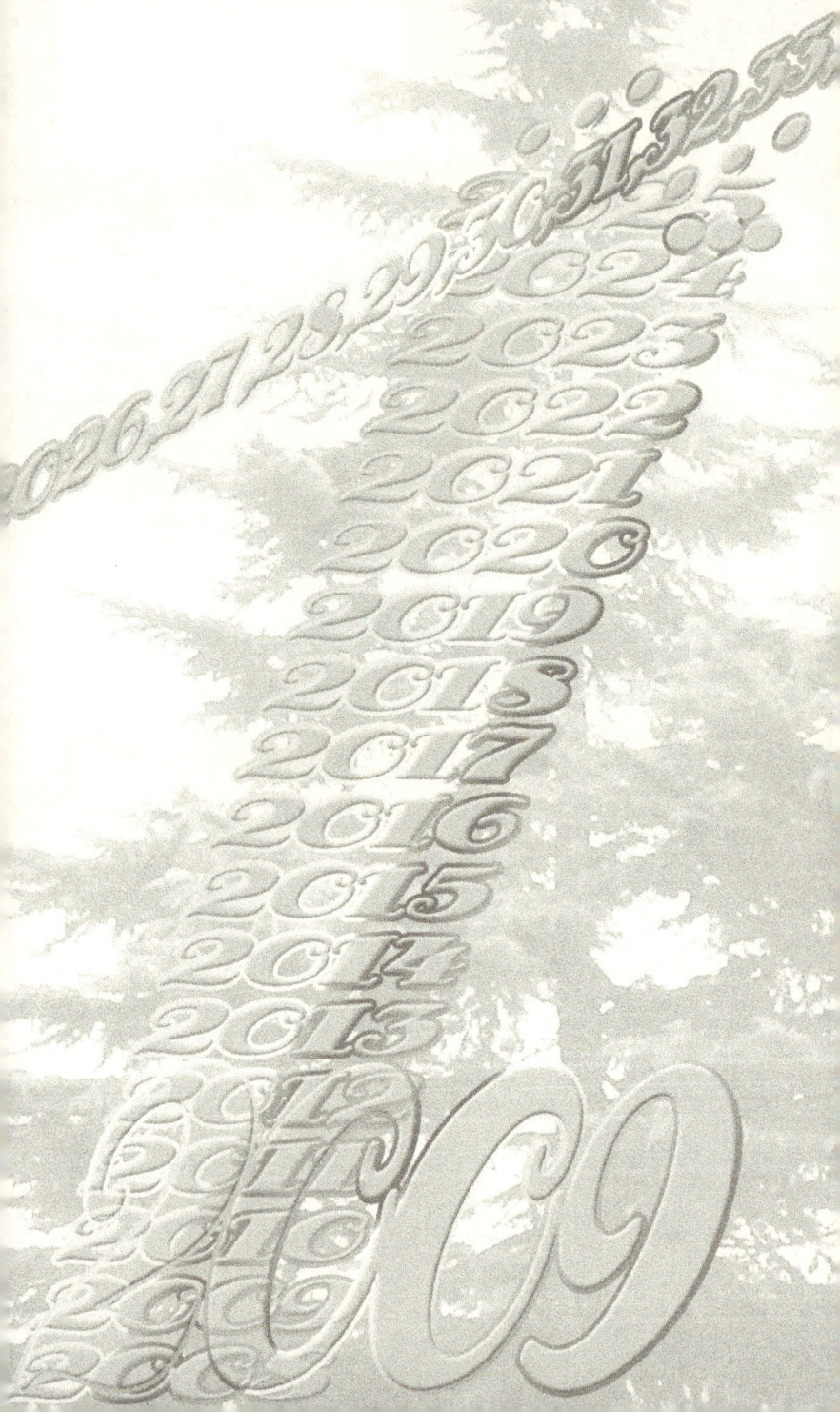

Time is life
smiling
upon
simple & true
self

Credit goes to
the team of designers,
photographers, cartoonists,
and editor Dean Goodluck
at the publisher: D'Moon

Copyright ©D'Moon
first edition, 2021
all rights reserved
except for reader comments and
poems & quotes not by LuCxeed

ISBN: 978-1-933187-87-7

Slight variations may occur
as part of the print-on-demand process
since each book is manufactured in its entirety.

Your feedback is most welcome ~
publisher@worldculturepictorial.com

Dan Goodluck

FIVE STEPS WISER

World Culture Pictorial
Reading & Reflection Vol. 05

Nimimm books

Weeping Sky
poem by LuCxeed

Deep into midnight, cry
in soundless silence. Sky
is weeping, tears falling so slow
frozen into crystal snow
to quiet down the around
in dark, laying mourning white

Unyielding. Eyes, half shut
speak oceans of unspoken
comprehended
by hands in hands
soaked in streaming tears
Time stolen. Heart, broken
whispers into departing Dearest's ears
"...can you hear me? remember
my love, uncompromising, will forever
walk beside you...anywhere...ever..."

"Hear ya –" outside
muffled echoes of broken heart, crying
tears falling from far above, so slow
frozen into crystal snow
Darkness solemnly wears mourning white
Sky weeping... deep midnight

Introduction

Life haunted in more than one year.
So halted the publication of
Five Steps Wiser.
To greet light breaking darkness,
lifting up curtains at horizon,
folks step out,
billions and billions,
pray for those fallen
"ashes to ashes, dust to dust",
thank the blessings for the spared,
wipe tears, be brave, carry on!
Be brave, cheer up for others around,
for those dear ones
watching us from Heaven.
Be brave, and cheer up!
Light at dawn breaks darkness
for all on the magnificent planet,
for a good day today,
for a better tomorrow.

When it comes to reading,
the leisure and pleasure of
holding a book in hand
is hardly replaced by electronics,
though smartphone gets smarter.

Online-and-offline learning
joins in a fine-art quality book,
Five Steps Wiser.
Each, of more than 100 selected entries,
is a glimpse through an invisible window,
leading to an amazing story, character,
or technology's surprising advancement.
Each entry offers a link for online
exploration (or relevant stunning photos:
half a house standing upright,
birds follow ultralight plane) –

first International Polar Year,
first electric telegraph,
first Macintosh innovation,
first to swim at North Pole,
first wish of George Washington,
first US Secretary of State,
first supersonic jetliner,
first Motor Race,
first indigenous President, Bolivia,
first Emperor BC, united China,
first heavy traffic wooden bridge,
        Netherlands,
first "Jumbo Hostel", a retired 747,
first kiss of love.

In print is also some readers' reflection,
a connection beyond the book,
beyond screen.
Readers' thoughtful comments
are truly inspiring
and halfway testimonials to bring
these books to more peoples
as the famous do many other books.
Another uniqueness of
Five Steps Wiser is to
bring classic poems into
modern life (Section II).

We are created with vision
without limitation
unless limited
by choices to learn less.
Knowledge
instills confidence
to be more prudent.
Day by day,
step by step,
we are wiser.

Publisher's Note

Life. Science. Nature.

Human has ambition, Science aggression. Earth passiveness, though, admittedly Nature's temper, now and then, here or there, can smash at all, everything in sight or in imagination backed up by the total of global fortune. Thus comes a quest: what is the origin, an origin the rest are resting upon? The classic thought as Sir Francis Bacon's is convenient yet convincing?

®

moon

"I.
MAN, being the servant and interpreter of Nature,
can do and understand so much and so much
only as he has observed in fact or in thought
of the course of nature: beyond this he neither
knows anything nor can do anything.

II.
Neither the naked hand nor the understanding
left to itself can effect much.
It is by instruments and helps that the work is done,
which are as much wanted for the understanding
as for the hand. And as the instruments of the hand
either give motion or guide it,
so the instruments of the mind supply either
suggestions for the understanding or cautions."

Had the beginning of The Interpretation Of Nature
offered a clue to the clueless, Life and Science'd have
a good head on shoulders, not over heels, resting
upon Earth. Fifth Step Wiser. Marvelous!

Dean Goodluck

Contents

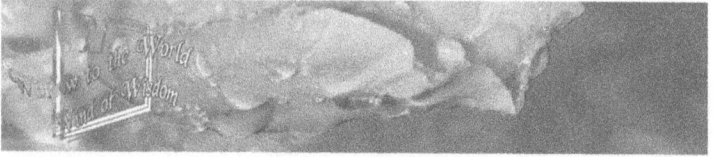

Section 1

Contents

Contents

Contents

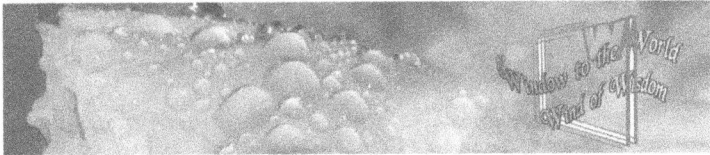

Contents

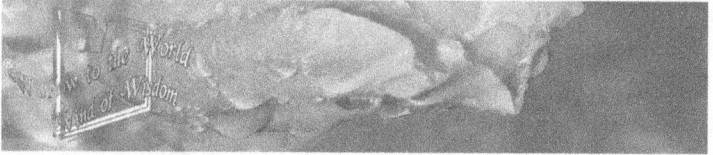

Contents

Dean Goodluck

Contents

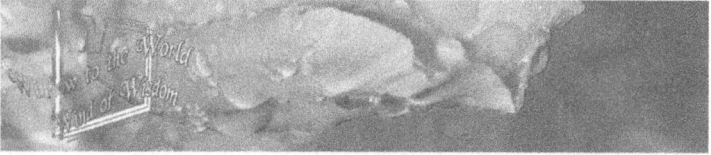

Contents

Dean Goodluck

Contents

Contents

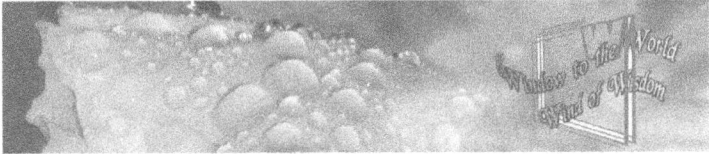

Contents

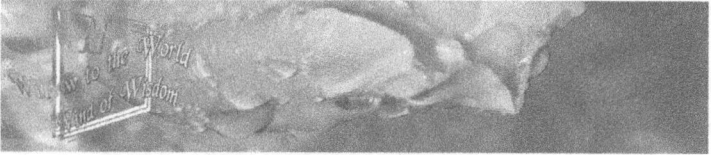

2009/02/10
Lord Byron
"Pleasure in the pathless woods;
rapture on the lonely shore
By the deep sea,
and music in its roar"

2009/02/11
newest republic
and century-old culture

2009/02/12
Photo: *grandpa in 80s*
with 9-year-old granddaughter

2009/02/13
Ocean Mysteries:
jellyfish reverting
to younger self

Contents

Dean Goodluck

Contents

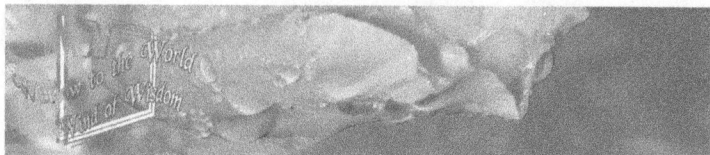

24

Contents

Dean Goodluck

Contents

2009/02/27
final Sherlock Holmes novel
by Sir Arthur Conan Doyle

2009/02/28
idealist believes the short run
cynic believes the long run
realist?

2009/03/01
tallest buildings
Taipei Tower 101
Burj Dubai & 1-km High Club

2009/03/02
Children's Film Festival
100 films from
30 countries

Contents

Dean Goodluck

Contents

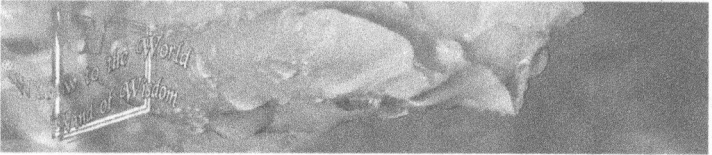

2009/03/06
Photography
Kenya
Elephants

2009/03/07
NASA
looking for
Earth's twin

2009/03/08
Einstein
on
the mysterious

2009/03/09
screaming "God, she fell in!"
he jumped down to the tracks
light coming into the tunnel

Contents

Dean Goodluck

Contents

Contents

2009/03/19
tea plantation
boundless green

2009/03/20
crisis in Europe

2009/03/21
"Conscience is God
present in man."
- Victor Hugo

2009/03/22
He looks out over tent city
as storm clouds gather above

2009/03/23
Robert Frost
"Her early leaf's a flower;
But only so an hour"

Contents

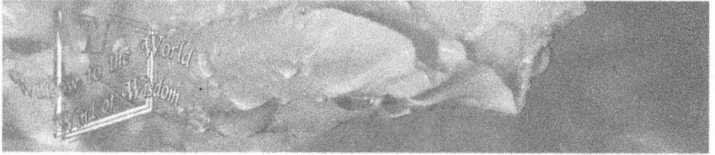

Contents

Dean Goodluck

Contents

Contents

Dean Goodluck

Contents

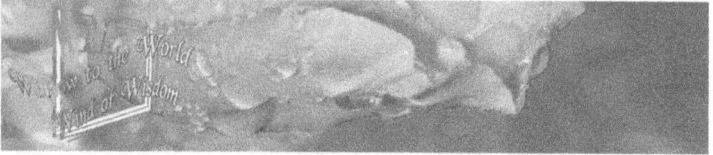

Contents

Dean Goodluck

Contents

Contents

Dean Goodluck

Contents

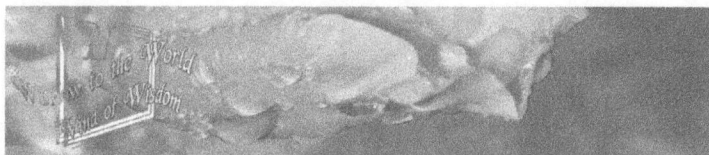

Contents

❄ ❄ ❄

World Culture Pictorial®
WcP Blog
Book Covers of Other Volumes
in the Series

Section

1

Dean Goodluck

www.worldculturepictorial.com/blog/archive/all/2009/01/01

Chuckles from the top of Everest

Love delivers kisses aplenty
so does lust or affection
so does scheme or infatuation
so does courtesy or flirtation

Among the plenty, the First Kiss
of love, prima of romance
crowned with a diamond crown
in the blaze of ever-sweet bliss

chuckles from the top of Everest
laughing at the rest
of romance fled
as Daylight browns the bedroom

14   23

2009 / 01 / 01
WcP.Poetic.Thought

Lyrical poem
by LuCxeed
"the First Kiss of love"

Chuckles from the Top of Everest
by LuCxeed

Love delivers kisses aplenty
so does lust or affection
so does scheme or infatuation
so does courtesy or flirtation

Among the plenty, the First Kiss
of love, prime of romance
crowned with a diamond crown
in the blaze of ever-sweet bliss

chuckles from the top of Everest
laughing at the rest
of romance fled
as Daylight brooms the bedroom

From pages 19 & 20 of the book: Love's
Footsteps ~ dedicated to a Bridge for
Wisdom to Walk on

Dean Goodluck

www.worldculturepictorial.com/blog/archive/all/2009/01/01

2009/01/01
WcP.Poetic.Thought

"Is Past a past or a ghost?"
Lyrical poem by LuCxeed
"Off the Train of Morrow"

"Is Past a past or a ghost?" - excerpt from poem "Off the Train of Morrow"
Excerpt from Off the Train of Morrow
by LuCxeed

Is Past a past
or a ghost?
Mind of Time, haunted,
disturbed, confused,
cannot think, nor rest...

From the book: Love's Footsteps ~
dedicated to a Bridge for Wisdom to Walk
on

Dean Goodluck

2009/01/02
WCP.System.Thinker

International Year of Astronomy
2009

135 countries committed to International Year of Astronomy 2009: "The Universe, yours to discover." Began on 1 Jan

www.worldculturepictorial.com/blog/archive/all/2009/01/02

2009/01/03
WcP.Humor

Nature's Wonder.
panda checks birthday cake
bear cub peeks out

Nature's Wonder. Photos: puffin touchdown, panda examines B-day cake, polar bear cub peeks out from mother's arms

www.worldculturepictorial.com/blog/archive/all/2009/01/03

Reader Comments

♦ 2017/10/20 - "Polar bears are marine warm blooded animals, and invest quite a bit of their energy in Arctic ocean ice. Numerous adjustments make polar bears extraordinarily suited to life in frosty natural surroundings. Their hide is thicker than some other bears' and covers even their feet for warmth and footing on ice."

Dean Goodluck

2009/01/04
WcP.Scientific.Mind

Mars rovers
Spirit & Opportunity

Amazing! Spirit & Opportunity, Mars rovers (expected lifespan of 90 days from Jan 3 '04), roving on into 5 yrs

www.worldculturepictorial.com/ blog/ archive/ all/ 2009/ 01/ 04

2009/01/05
WcP.Common.Sense

It is curious that physical courage should be so common in the world and moral courage so rare.

"It is curious that physical courage should be so common in the world and moral courage so rare."
- Mark Twain

www.worldculturepictorial.com/blog/archive/all/2009/01/05

Dean Goodluck

2009/01/06
WCP.Scientific.Mind

Samuel Morse
1st electric telegraph
"What hath God wrought!"

Jan 6, 1838, Samuel Morse 1st demonstrated electric telegraph. "What hath God wrought!" - 1st formal message sent

www.worldculturepictorial.com/blog/archive/all/2009/01/06

Reader Comments

(not in chronological order)

♦ 2012/03/13 – "Many communication systems and devices can owe their start to Samuel Morse. I think he was the first one that demonstrated that messages can be transmitted almost instantaneously. This idea translated into the mobile phones, text messages and emails that we know of today."

♦ 2012/11/07 - "That's very true, if it wasn't for the creation of the electrical telegraph we might not even have landlines let alone mobile phones! This is the same for many first inventions, if it wasn't for those inventors - whom many people thought where crazy at the time - we might not be where we are with today's technology, just think how much better off we all are now thanks to so many inventors!"

♦ 2012/02/21 - "It must have been quite a technological leap at that time for telecommunication. Before the telegraph, detailed messages could not be sent between two distances in such a short time. People relied on horseback delivery or even homing pigeon to transmit messages. All telephones and even mobile phones owe their start to that humble device."

♦ 2017/02/14 - "History gives us a lot of lessons. I think that our task is to study it and to understand the reasons and consequences. Thank you for this amazing article. I enjoyed reading it."

♦ 2012/11/19 – "I found this blog to be very interesting and helpful as the fact it helped me to see how far along technology had come since the beginning in term of how financially rewarding it was as well."

♦ 2014/10/31 – "It is really a nice and helpful piece of information. I am satisfied that you just shared this useful info with us. Please keep us informed like this. Thanks for sharing."

♦ 2018/09/03 – "Many thanks for sharing with us, I always find out something new from your posts."

2009/01/07
WcP.System.Thinker

Solar system moving faster
than thought
15% speed increase

Solar system moving 100000 mph faster than thought; 15% speed increase translates to doubling of mass of Milky Way

www.worldculturepictorial.com/blog/archive/all/2009/01/07

Reader Comments

(not in chronological order)

♦ 2013/08/10 - "In Awe... Mind-boggling read. As our human understanding of the world around us increases, the Universe seems to possess an untold number of secrets."

♦ 2013/05/14 - "I think solar power is the answer for everything in the future."

- 2012/06/17 - "So what happens when you point a beam of light in the exact direction the solar system is traveling; and then the opposite direction? It would seem to me that there would be a 0.0847% to .1694% speed (red shift) difference since a beam of light cannot travel faster than the speed of light."

- 2012/05/10 - "I Love The F=MV. Although, even if the milky way weighs more, I suppose it doesn't matter.
However, its really fascinating, and I'm glad you threw it into the title. Really eye-catching, there. Now, if we could only use all of this energy in a positive way that meets our practical needs - such as making use of Solar Power's Advantages, we might have something truly worth "writing home" about.
ET, Phone Home?"

- 2013/12/09 - "It's not the heat but the sunlight that produce electricity, 21 June, when we we get maximum solar energy in the northern hemisphere, but other factors, such as the clouds make a difference too."

♦ 2009/09/08 - "Solar energy is the future while other sources of renewable energy will be kind of complementary. The information about solar system is very interesting and also useful for me. Thanks to author..."

♦ 2011/09/26 - "I truly believe that, even though I'm sure solar energy will play a pivotal role, it is regeneration and kinetic energy that will eventually be the better option for renewable energy sources. I have come to appreciate Nikola Tesla's invention of the "mechanical oscillator", and believe it will be possible to use "cosmic rays" to our advantage."

♦ 2017/08/11 - "Hats off to astronomers who do a tremendous job. salute to their efforts."

♦ 2017/02/28 - "Wow... wow... wow and all of that newfound bulk is composed of dark matter."

♦ 2013/07/01 - "I think it's all quite interesting stuff, but I don't see how it helps us as a people. I'm more into discoveries that can advance the human race, rather than ones that appear to be undertaken out of interest."

♦ 2012/07/26 - "Do I have your approval to use some of the information from your article in a school project?"

- 2018/05/31 - "This specific spiral galaxy is labeled a grand design galaxy as it has prominent and shapely spiral arms."
- 2017/11/14 - "Wow, does it really happen? if so, it's really incredible."
- 2017/06/06 - "The space experts say that the way that this cosmic system exists is surprising. The researchers take note of that ebb and flow intelligence trusted that such winding systems didn't exist at such an early time ever."
- 2015/04/22 - "I think scientists and astronomers are making a great effort in this regard and this discovery (I call it a great success, not just discovery) will make us realize these things will continue to bear fruit."
- 2015/06/09 - "Yes you are right, i agree with your point."
- 2016/03/06 - "WOW it's unbelievable Solar system's moving 100000 mph faster ??!!!! How is it possible?? I am thinking a lot but no answer..... Classy"
- 2012/10/15 - "When i was young, my favorite subject is about the solar system. I feel so interested about our solar system."

- 2012/10/29 - "Can I know how do we come to know abt the speed of the moving galaxy? and what is the end to it?"
- 2013/07/01 - "I've always had an interest in space exploration, but discoveries like these, I'd like to see where they're going with this."
- 2013/06/15 - "Well scientific era make it soon easy..."
- 2013/09/15 - "How do you foresee that to change our own planet?"
- 2018/11/22 - "Nice work, bookmarking it."
- 2012/01/18 - "Generally I do not post on blogs, but I would like to say that this post really forced me to do so, Excellent post!"
- 2013/07/28 - "I have never read of anything like this and it is interesting to know. It's amazing how you find out things like this and it changes everything previously known about it."
- 2012/07/12 - "I have been assigned to do a report for our school newspaper on this subject, and your post has been beneficial. Can you please add more reference to this topic, thanks."
- 2014/01/17 - "I am really enjoying reading your well written article. I think you spend numerous effort and time updating your blog."

- 2016/11/16 – "Our planet turns on its axis once a day. I explain with example here: When we are on an easily riding train, we occasionally get the delusion that the train is standing still and the buildings are moving backwards. In the same way, because we 'ride' with the turning Earth, it performs to us that the Sun and the stars are the ones doing the moving as day and night alternate. But actually, it is our planet that turns on its axis once a day and all of us who live on the Earth's surface are moving with it."
- 2017/03/02 – "Couldn't be written any better. Reading this post reminds me of my old roommate! He always kept talking about this."
- 2018/09/09 – "Excellent post. I am happy to get the chance to read such a well-written article."
- 2017/07/17 – "By knowing the speed of solar system feels great. It also tells us that it would take no longer time for gravity. We are evolving day by day in the technology field."
- 2013/08/12 – "This is really a fascinating blog, lots of stuff that I can get into. One thing I just want to say is that your blog is so perfect!"

- 2017/03/21 - "I hope next time when i visit here you will share marvelous stuff too like this. Good to be here and to read this amazing article."

- 2015/09/08 - "Nice level of information here. There is certainly so much data around about Solar System that sometimes you cannot see the wood for the trees but you could have pitched this at just the proper level so that the lay individual can understand - thank you!"

- 2012/07/31 - "I totally agreed with this fact it is such an informative article. Thanks for writing this good post."

- 2012/09/03 - "I totally agree with you!"

- 2012/08/13 - "Me too, this article is very informative, it helps me understand how small we are in the entire Universe. Amazing!"

- 2018/01/08 - "Thanks for each outstanding post that will be others. Otherwise may just anyone get that kind of guidance in such a perfect manner of authorship?"

- 2017/07/04 - "Great post. Very major concepts are clear after reading this wonderful post. A great thanks for this useful information. Keep blogging."

- 2015/04/23 – "This is an awesome post. Really very informative and creative. This sharing of concept is a good way to enhance knowledge. Thank you very much for this post. I like this site very much."

- 2018/01/08 – "I have recommended this to pals and my relatives and loved reading your post. Your website is extraordinary and I will be likely to keep on urging it to my buddies."

- 2012/10/02 – "For me, the solar system is the most beautiful to discover and observe because it has a lot of white colors."

- 2018/01/08 – "This may be a place that is awesome. Your layout is wholly distinct as I want to convey to others which you only are carrying out a job that is amazing."

- 2018/01/08 – "You happen to be a superb writer I love you post. Excellent article rather illustrative post this is. I'll be waiting for another one."

- 2018/04/02 – "Nice and very informative post. Thanks to share with us. Happy to Read."

- 2017/11/23 – "I am actually amazed with your initiatives as well as actually pleased to see this post."

◆ 2017/11/18 - "Such a nice post, keep up the fantastic work."

◆ 2017/11/18 - "Appreciate the information published on the blog keep on posting new things."

◆ 2017/11/13 - "I really appreciate the kind of topics you post here. Thanks for sharing great information about solar system that is actually helping my great pleasure to visit your blog and to enjoy your great posts here."

◆ 2017/03/14 - "Very Informative post you gave to us, really helpful. I would like to share something really helpful for education."

◆ 2017/09/01 - "Very interesting information, keep on sharing. It's very hard to be a good writer. First of all, one must be very skillful and educated. "

◆ 2017/08/11 - "This post helps me to gain important information about the solar system. Til now I was not aware of the speed and weight relationship of the solar system but this completely describes this relationship."

◆ 2017/11/12 - "I really love your dedication in your post..."

◆ 2017/08/11 - "We are very busy in our daily life and unaware about this news. Thanks to you who posts these kinds of articles."

- 2017/07/25 - "The mass of Milky Way is always greater and the planets around them are in orbit to evolve about the sun in order to give the best rotational shift."

- 2017/07/24 - "It is a wonderful post. Thanks for sharing this. It will provide us knowledge about this topic."

- 2017/07/24 - "Wow! It's an amazing blog, I liked your post well, discussion on how our Galaxy works. Thanks for sharing a nice post."

- 2017/07/21 - "Simply desire to say your article is astonishing. The clearness in your post is simply spectacular and i can assume you're an expert on this subject. Thanks a million and please carry on the rewarding work."

- 2017/07/04 - "Thanks a lot for sharing it, that truly has added a lot to our knowledge about this topic. Have a more successful day."

- 2017/06/11 - "Amazing universe. I was so amazed when I realize our wonderful world. I am so delighted to be here."

- 2017/05/31 - "I greatly appreciate this article."

- 2017/03/31 - "Admin has excellent way to teach by blog... thanks for informative post..."

- 2017/03/09 - "I am very happy to read this. This is the kind of manual that needs to be given and not the random misinformation that's at other blogs. Appreciate your sharing this best posting."
- 2017/01/18 - "The information and the detail were just perfect. I think that your perspective is deep, it's just well thought out and really fantastic to see someone who knows how to put these thoughts down so well."
- 2016/12/01 - "Great! Love reading such articles which are tough to find these days."
- 2016/09/22 - "I agree with you. It's really awesome blog on Solar system."
- 2017/05/04 - "Very enjoyable Thank you."
- 2016/04/14 - "Wow..... Interesting Post."
- 2016/03/01 - "Nice blog and absolutely outstanding. You can do something much better but i still say this is perfect. Keep trying for the best."
- 2015/11/09 - "A great work has been done. I liked this blog post."
- 2016/06/10 - "I love this post, it's amazing."
- 2015/06/10 - "Nice effort for nice post. Well done."

- 2015/03/08 – "Fantastic post from you, man. I have kept in mind your stuff previously too and you're simply extremely excellent. I really like what you've brought right here, really like what you are stating and the best way by which you assert it."

- 2015/03/09 – "'Sun' is inevitable by 'Solar', the organization here is how the planets are thoroughly spinning around a sun in the centre. you shouldn't mix up between a galaxy and a solar organization. A galaxy is when solar arrangements revolve around a single black gap together."

- 2015/01/11 – "I found the perfect place for my needs. Contains wonderful and useful messages. I have read most of them and has a lot of them."

- 2015/01/29 – "Really helpful and really awesome! I wish I could be out there some day!"

- 2014/11/25 – "Your website is very nice and very interesting."

- 2014/09/10 – "I always love to read about solar system, all i want to read exists in this blog."

♦ 2012/12/08 - "Fantastic information about solar system... The Solar System consists of the Sun and the astronomical objects bound to it by gravity, all of which formed from the collapse of a giant molecular cloud... thanks"

♦ 2013/07/31 - "Good! This post is creative, you'll find a lot of new ideas, it gives me inspiration. I believe I will also be inspired by you and feel extra new ideas. Thanks"

♦ 2013/05/16 - "I just found this blog and have high hopes for it to continue.I believe this really is excellent information. Thanks for sharing. "

♦ 2013/05/25 - "I have been searching for quite some time for information on this topic and no doubt your website saved my time and I got my desired information. Your post has been very helpful. Thanks."

♦ 2012/11/26 - "This is the right blog for anyone who wants to find out about this topic. You realize so much it's almost hard to argue with you (not that I actually would want to... HaHa). You definitely put a new spin on a topic that's been written about for years. Great stuff, just great!"

- 2012/08/15 – "This post has been extremely insightful and useful to increase my knowledge in the field of knowledge and its many facets. Thank you very much, I will certainly come back to visit often and definitely tell some of my internet-inclined friends to visit this site. Keep posting and expressing your knowledge and opinions strong!"

- 2012/06/15 – "Really great post, brightly written article, if only all bloggers open the same level of content as you, the internet would be a much better place."

- 2012/05/17 – "Your blog is very impressive!! Nice post. This is the way I like to see informational content written. This post is different from what I read on most blogs. And it has so many valuable things to learn. Thank you for your sharing!"

- 2012/05/12 – "Wow, awesome post, I am wondering, and found your site by Google, learned a lot, now I'm a bit clear. Bookmarked and also signed up your site. Keep us updated...thanks"

- 2011/12/17 - "I just want to say that it's my favorite topic for searching and reading and after reading your blog post about it i have no need for more searching and reading."
- 2013/04/01 - "Fantastic post, thank you very much!"
- 2013/04/23 - "It is such a great resource that you're providing and you also give it away for nothing. I love seeing websites that understand the worthiness of providing a prime resource for free. I truly loved reading your post. Thanks!"
- 2012/08/03 - "I'm definitely sure the visitors who visit your site will like your content and pointers."
- 2012/06/29 - "I have enjoyed this so much. This was a great and fun informational article. Thanks so much."
- 2012/07/23 - "Thanks for help me by sharing this and i will share this to my friends and keep it up!"

2009/01/08
WCP.Story.Teller

Lewis Gordon Pugh
1st to swim at North Pole

Lewis Gordon Pugh, real and very first person to swim at North Pole? Astonishing! Earth has fever?

www.worldculturepictorial.com/blog/archive/all/2009/01/08

Reader Comments

♦ 2010/09/17 - "Nice pic! I don't know if I can swim in that water! You're very brave."

♦ 2010/11/02 - "I know I wouldn't be capable of doing it! Very brave indeed."

♦ 2010/11/11 - "Jeez. I would freeze in there. Also, I cannot swim so, what would I do once I was inside? Scream like a lady?"

♦ 2010/11/19 - "I know for sure I wouldn't be able to swim in those waters either! Like the pic a lot though."

♦ 2013/04/12 - "This is one awesome blog.Thanks Again. Much obliged."

2009/01/09
WcP.Poetic.Thought

we should ourselves complain

A wretched soul, bruised with adversity,
We bid be quiet when we hear it cry;
But were we burdened with like weight of pain,
As much or more
we should ourselves complain.

- William Shakespeare

www.worldculturepictorial.com/ blog/ archive/ all/ 2009/01/09

2009/01/10
WcP.Observer

Africa
wooden bikes

Bikes including wooden bikes help break poverty trap - many Africans spend 4 hrs/day walking, 1/4 income on transport

www.worldculturepictorial.com/blog/archive/all/2009/01/10

Reader Comments

- ◆ 2016/03/29 - "Very nice."
- ◆ 2016/11/26 - "I really love bikes! In fact, I travel the world on it!"
- ◆ 2016/11/27 - "Perth is one of the most interesting and picturesque places and what better way to explore this amazing City than from a bike."

Dean Goodluck

2009/01/11
WcP.Art

Mastery of Winter
Skaters or the swan?
International Ice & Snow Show

Mastery of Winter. Onto ice are skaters, swan, crabapple tree, children and sculptures at International Ice and Snow Show

www.worldculturepictorial.com/blog/archive/all/2009/01/11

2009/01/12
WcP.WatchfulEye

Peru, a poor nation to plant 40 million trees

Peru, one of poorest countries with 30% population living <$2, 10% <$1 a day, to plant 40 million trees by Feb '20

www.worldculturepictorial.com/blog/archive/all/2009/01/12

Dean Goodluck

2009 / 01 / 13
WCP.Life.Coach

The strongest principle of growth
lies in the human choice.

"The strongest principle of growth
lies in the human choice."
- George Eliot

www.worldculturepictorial.com/blog/archive/all/2009/01/13

2009/01/14
WcP.Story.Teller

World's tallest buildings (part ii): Washington Monument, Eiffel Tower

World's tallest buildings (part ii): Washington Monument, Eiffel Tower, Chrysler Building, Empire State Building...

www.worldculturepictorial.com/blog/archive/all/2009/01/14

Reader Comments

(not in chronological order)

◆ 2017/04/28 – "Nice article. Humans had been always fascinated by the heights and this fascination and the mind to reach greater heights paved the way for skyscrapers like these. Now it's has turned out to be a competition between countries to build the tallest structure ever made by humans."

- 2017/11/20 – "These buildings are art pieces of architecture and design. You shared amazing information with high quality writing. Thanks a lot."

- 2016/10/19 – "Just Wow! These tall highest buildings in USA are so beautiful to see through eye. It had a great experience for everyone."

- 2015/12/23 – "These seven are really the most beautiful creation of the architect. As per my view, The Petronas Towers of Malaysia is the most attractive. Though, it takes long time to complete such infrastructures but the foundation should be made strong and with the perfect measurement. Awaiting the next amazing blogs with some more interesting infrastructures!"

- 2017/10/13 – "What I think now is that Burj Khalifa now holds the title.. Any guess which one is coming next??"

- 2015/11/24 – "Best view in DC – we visited the monument several times on our trip, day and night. Night time was my favorite time."

- 2013/11/15 – "These building look awesome, I visited a couple of them and I liked it."

- 2017/11/22 – "Thanks for sharing. I love to go Eiffel Tower."

- 2013/05/20 - "There many mega structures that man has created. Here are some of the world's tallest buildings. These are very much amazing to see and it attracts the onlookers. I have got a very good read on the topic."

- 2012/05/10 - "The buldings look great. I have a lot of respect for the arhitects and the people involved in their construction. I saw how much work it is only for building a small home, I can't even imagine what it took to build all this impressive constructions."

- 2013/11/15 - "I travel a lot, I have visited a lot of cities from North Carolina and all of them were great. My oldest son likes a lot the Chrysler building, in his opinion this building has the best design from all the skyscrapers."

- 2018/11/29 - "In this post, you put great information indeed, keep sharing."

- 2018/09/18 - "Informative Blog!! I loved the post, keep posting interesting posts. I will be a regular reader..."

- 2018/12/20 - "Nice post."

- 2016/10/20 - "Thanks for sharing informative content."

♦ 2012/02/23 – "Personally, I dislike man's race for building the tallest structure in the world. There is not much point in doing so, except to boast the country's economic progress, or to make a statement. The amount of construction materials that go into building those tall buildings would be better spent on improving the living conditions or providing new homes for the less fortunate. It seems to me, that the taller the structure, the greater the presence of greed."

♦ 2012/09/17 – "Seriously, seriously? Wow."

♦ 2012/03/21 – "They build it not just to build. Every structure has its assignment."

♦ 2015/03/31 – "Excellent goods from you, man. I have understood your stuff previously too and you are just extremely excellent. I really like what you have acquired here, certainly like what you're saying and the way in which you say it. You make it enjoyable and you still care to keep it smart. I can't wait to read much more from you. This is really a terrific site."

2009/01/15
WcP.Story.Teller

Mike Horn
4-year 7-continent eco-voyage

Around the world in 1460 days: Mike Horn navigates sustainable sailboat Pangaea on 4-year 7-continent eco-voyage

www.worldculturepictorial.com/blog/archive/all/2009/01/15

2009/01/16
WCP.Philosophy

In the fields of observation chance favors only those minds which are prepared.

"In the fields of observation chance favors only those minds which are prepared."
- Louis Pasteur

www.worldculturepictorial.com/blog/archive/all/2009/01/16

2009 /01/17
WcP.Art

Bailouts for museums?

Art, space, but no benefactors
U.S. museums look inward for their own
bailouts

www.worldculturepictorial.com/blog/archive/all/2009/01/17

Dean Goodluck

2009/01/18
WcP.Observer

3rd-largest economy

China becomes world's third-largest economy with 13% '07 GDP growth, surpassing Germany and closing rapidly on Japan

www.worldculturepictorial.com/blog/archive/all/2009/01/18

2009/01/19
WcP.Scientific.Mind

Magical 15 seconds from car to aircraft

From car to aircraft in 15 seconds: 'roadable' plane Terrafugia Transition is a flying car that fits in the garage

www.worldculturepictorial.com/ blog/ archive/ all/ 2009/01/19

Reader Comments

(not in chronological order)

♦ 2013/04/25 – "Where can I buy it? I want this car! Is it already in sale??"

♦ 2013/06/05 – "This is all very new to me and this article really opened my eyes. New car. Cool. I really wish I hadn't seen this as I really want one now!"

♦ 2012/05/10 - "I can say that I'm very surprised. I never heard about this type of car or plane. It's a great idea. I wonder what kind of axle assembly it has and how much it costs if it breaks."

♦ 2012/12/08 - "I didn't hear neither. I think it's amazing. I only saw it on the SF movies. Having this type of car in my garage will be great."

♦ 2012/08/26 - "With the rising fuel prices, it will become more and more expensive to pilot one of these things in the future. Assuming someone has the funds to buy it, and also of course has the time to get the license to pilot it."

♦ 2012/07/19 - "'Roadable' plane... Or do you think it is going to be just a leisure aircraft? Do you see it 'taking off' and leading to flying cars? I moved away from a scenario ten years ago and don't want my family having it easier to get to me. Am I just being paranoid?"

♦ 2013/03/24 - "This flying car design is quite brilliant, but I'm not sure how practical it is. I first saw a picture of it in the local newspaper... I thought to myself 'who would drive such a contraption?' or better yet, who would drive it and fly it?"

♦ 2013/04/03 - "This flying car can be quite practical, Robyn. I live in West Maine and in order to get to work every day I need to cross a crowded bridge that's often closed due to the bad weather. A car like this one could be a life saver for me and other people in my situation."

♦ 2012/04/06 - "From car to aircraft... That's great!!! First time I heard about this and I am shocked. Is it true? How did they make and have the same parts as the normal car. Such a great vehicle with good transition, safety cage and beautiful design."

♦ 2011/07/20 - "What makes me curious is how would a driver switch from driving to flying and if the driver requires a 'flying license'. Probably not the flying car I imagined way back in high school and I wonder if I would see one in any luxury car rental in the future."

♦ 2015/05/20 - "Your post is very useful and very informative. It's my pleasure to reach this post for getting best information and increasing my knowledge."

◆ 2012/03/20 - "Wow, look at this. From aircraft to car? How did they make this kind of vehicle? Awesome. Does this vehicle have the same parts as the normal car like let say, transmission parts and brakes parts? Does this run on the same fuel? Innovation has gone beyond people's imagination. This is a proof of that. I can see the future is very bright ahead of us."

◆ 2012/05/23 - "Honestly, there are no flying cars yet in our country and I haven't heard or seen anyone has it. I am sure only those billionaires can afford to buy this one. But honestly too, we don't know that there is also much traffic in the sky nowadays the same as almost the traffic in the land."

◆ 2012/12/25 - "I wish to show my thanks to the creator of this blog. Keep contributing good concepts and strategies. Many people will surely improve their skills by reading blogs like this."

◆ 2016/04/27 - "I'm still learning from you, but I'm trying to achieve my goals. I certainly enjoy reading all that is written on your site. Keep the articles coming. I enjoyed it!"

◆ 2016/05/30 - "Great writing, it is such a good and nice idea thanks."

♦ 2016/03/21 - "There are two primary reasons. One is that the innovation is basically based off a framework (oil, gas, and streets) that makes it really simple to construct a marginally better auto and make benefits. So the 'need' hasn't been sufficiently high to make it worth while for extensive financial specialists to make flying autos."

♦ 2016/03/21 - "Electronically monitored slowing mechanisms were initially created for air ships. An early framework was Dunlap's Maxaret framework, presented in the 1950s and still being used on some air ship models. This was a completely mechanical framework. It saw restricted car use in the 1960s in the Ferguson P99 dashing auto, the Jensen FF and the exploratory all wheel drive Ford Zodiac, however saw no further utilization; the framework demonstrated was costly and, in car use, fairly questionable."

♦ 2016/04/11 - "Thanks for sharing this nice blog. I read it completely and get some interesting content. I am waiting for your new blog please share new information. Thanks a lot..."

2009/01/20
WCP.Philosophy

George Washington's first wish

"My first wish is to see this plague of mankind, war, banished from the earth."
- George Washington

www.worldculturepictorial.com/blog/archive/all/2009/01/20

2009/01/21
WcP.Tomorrows.History

Remaking America
in which way?

Obama takes office, calling to join him "in the work of remaking America." Future history will see: in which way?

www.worldculturepictorial.com/blog/archive/all/2009/01/21

2009/01/22
WCP.System.Thinker

Antarctica
Larsen B ice shelf

Antarctica: Larsen B ice shelf, a large floating ice mass shattered, separated: AVHRRadiometer deployed on satellites since 1981

www.worldculturepictorial.com/blog/archive/all/2009/01/22

Reader Comments

♦ 2009/01/24 – "Thanks for keeping it real!"

2009 / 01 / 23
WcP.Scientific.Mind

*first Macintosh
innovation in
a quarter century*

25 years of innovation: Apple's unveiling of the first Macintosh forever changed the future of personal computing

www.worldculturepictorial.com / blog / archive / all / 2009 / 01 / 23

Reader Comments

◆ 2012/03/24 – "I wonder if Apple's legacy and future will be at their best now that Steve Jobs passed away. His vision and everything that he had done really changed the way we see computers and phones today. So the team back there at Apple will really have to try to make the team be as good and great as before."

- 2012/03/26 – "This is the biggest company in the computers industry in my opinion. I read about the rising number of apps available for the iPhone and iPad. The way this company evolved and they changed the way we see the computer today is simply amazing."
- 2012/08/02 – "I'm a big fan of Apple's. It's amazing how they could play with the technology."
- 2012/03/24 – "The history of Apple is fantastic. Steve Jobs started from nothing, he even didn't graduate and look how far he went. I am a big Apple fan, I am the proud owner of an iPhone and an iPad. Buying apps is my favorite hobby. Mostly I am interested in strategy games."
- 2017/08/13 – "Apple Rocks!! This is one of the biggest company in the computers industry in the world. Thanks For Sharing such a beautiful article. Also Heavy Use of Computers can cause sleep issues."
- 2017/09/05 – "Great Articles. Thank's for sharing."

♦ 2012/01/05 – "Beginning with version 10.5 'Leopard' in late 2007, Mac OS X has shipped with native virtual desktop support, called Spaces, which allows up to 16 hosted virtual desktops. It allows the user to associate applications with a particular 'Space'. As of Mac OS X 10.7 'Lion', this functionality has been moved into Mission Control. Scrolling desktops were made available to Macintosh users by a 3rd party extension called Stepping Out created by Wes Boyd (the future founder of Berkeley Systems) in 1986."

♦ – "Technology has evolved a lot since 1984. Although not many of us remember the first computers, they revolutionized the market at that time. Now things have changed, we use digital voice recorders and smartphones on a daily basis. Gadgets make our lives easier, so why not take advantage of them?"

♦ 2017/12/30 – "Very good article."

♦ 2015/10/09 – "Thanks, this blog is very useful, i want to read again and again..."

2009/01/24
WcP.Humor

Life a tragedy or a comedy?

"The world is a tragedy to those who feel,
but a comedy to those who think."
- Jean de La Bruyere
(16 August 1645 – 11 May 1696)
French philosopher and moralist,
who was noted for his satire

www.worldculturepictorial.com/ blog/ archive/ all/ 2009/ 01/ 24

2009/01/25
WcP.Movie.Critic

renaissance man
Viggo Mortensen
on poetry, painting,
photography and music

10 questions for Viggo Mortensen, Golden Globe and Academy Award-nominated actor and renaissance man

www.worldculturepictorial.com/blog/archive/all/2009/01/25

Reader Comments

♦ 2016/11/22 – "Viggo Mortensen is my favorite actor and he plays different roles. Viggo Mortensen has also won a Golden Globe Award and he is an action hero in film industry."

♦ 2016/11/21 – "Thank you so much."

Dean Goodluck

2009 / 01 / 26
WcP.Art

Year of the Ox

Happy Lunar New Year! Especially to those born or to be born in the Year of the Ox

www.worldculturepictorial.com / blog / archive / all / 2009 / 01 / 26

2009/01/27
WcP.Story.Teller

A newborn
looking at you
without fear

A newborn giraffe, on the very first day, looking at the world without fear, but innocent curiosity

www.worldculturepictorial.com/blog/archive/all/2009/01/27

Reader Comments

♦ 2016/11/22 - "What an elegant article it is and the animal that we can see in this article is also looking so innocent. It required a lot of effort as we can judge how much hard work is done on the article for making it elegant and nice blog that would be liked by people."

2009/01/28
WCP.WatchfulEye

"SOS Amazon"
rainforests diminished
every second

"SOS Amazon": every second we lose 1.5 acres of rainforests once covering 14% of earth land surface, now a mere 6%

www.worldculturepictorial.com/blog/archive/all/2009/01/28

Reader Comments

(not in chronological order)

♦ 2014/05/22 – 'The Amazon River is really beautiful. The pictures of those insects are exceptional. I have never seen most of them. We must protect these animals and the forest at any cost. We must encourage and support communities and organizations like these.'

♦ 2018/03/22 – 'And what now? Now we see news about last northern white rhinoceros...'

♦ 2011/10/03 - 'If only the timber companies
  could open their eyes and see what rainforests
  can bring to the earth. I understand that there
  are mouths to feed, but according to the experts,
  they could make more money if they found other
  ways to harvest the renewable sources of foods in
  the forest! Even in this age of computers, the rate
  of deforestation still hasn't slowed, and we will
  continue to lose precious forests and animals if
  this doesn't stop.'

♦ 2015/07/20 - 'It is alarming how fast our
  rainforests are disappearing. However, I did the
  math, and if your estimate of 1.5 acres lost per
  second was literally true, we would destroy
  47,304,000 acres in only 1 year.
  (I got to that number by multiplying 1.5 x 60 sec.
  x 1 hour x 24 hrs x 365 days)
  The Nature Conservancy says that today we
  have 75 million acres of rainforest worldwide.
  Please let me know if I am misinterpreting
  something.
  Thank you,
  Murry'

♦ 2016/06/12 - 'Incredible post. This makes me
  think how much we harm our nature.'

- 2015/10/05 – 'This is a very nice article and the sad thing is that these days humans have only one thing in mind, MONEY. This greed has led them astray and they do what ever they deem fit for themselves. They don't care about what harm they are bringing to the world. Everyone should go for recycling.'
- 2014/12/24 – 'Rain forests are our planet's lungs, are our clean air, though it is quite polluted now and normal citizens never tried to breathe really fresh air… Sad this is…'
- 2015/06/08 – 'Amazing pictures.'
- 2015/03/03 – 'Develop or destroy? One side the development and other side destroying the environment has been more nowadays.'
- 2013/08/25 – 'It's bad news. Your article tells me a serious fact. Thanks for your share. Your pictures are so beautiful. I hope more and more people will notice the problem of amazon rainforest and pretect our only Earth. It's a great blog article about this topic.'
- 2013/09/17 – 'That is really some sad news. I hope people will start protecting it.'

- 2013/05/19 - 'This is really alarming, We must do something to protect these animals. '
- 2013/01/23 - 'This is very very important info on this subject, the amazonas as well as other source of oxygen for the planet have been removed by rich people to get richer.'
- 2012/11/20 - 'All these animals is nature. Our earth can be such colourful due to this original ecology. Protect the animal is to protect our colourful world.'
- 2013/01/22 - 'This is just something to be ashamed of, we humans have to change our behaviors towards our home called nature. Look at this situation with new fresh eyes.'
- 2012/07/27 - 'Good Job! This layout of losing this scads rainforest is pretty depressing, and it's such a big issue it's hard to know where to start.'
- 2013/04/18 - ':(I wish the people will learn how to protect Mother Nature. It's for their own good.'
- 2013/08/23 - 'That is really some sad information. The world has to realize this.'

♦ 2012/05/24 – "This is true and we are using the forest surface for living and for cultivation... this is not right."

♦ 2011/04/09 – "This idea of losing this much rainforest is pretty depressing, and it's such a big issue it's hard to know where to start. Can it be saved?"

♦ 2011/06/23 – "Well – we are a group who is working on it! We have created a project based upon an idea developed by the group IPCC, who won the Nobel Prize in 2007, along with Al Gore, for their innovative plan of how to save the rainforests, it's people, plants and animals – by becoming CO_2 neutral.
If you want to know more about it, check out our website. We can act! We CAN do something! And we have to hurry!! The more people who know about this possibility – the better for our Earth and the coming generations!
Greetings,
Kirsten Brabrand
Denmark"

♦ 2011/02/11 – "This is a great idea. We really need to implement rain forest for the further generations. This is a very good implementation."

- 2013/10/03 - "Thanks for sharing. I really appreciate it that you shared with us such an informative post and very easy to understand. We humans should definitely come forward and take some steps to save our environment as it gives us oxygen to survive and even there are more benefits of Nature in the Humans Life."

- 2013/10/26 - "It's unfortunate that this is happening, but the reality is that this was inevitable...a society built on materialism and greed, there was only one path for the rest of the world. So what is the solution? There isn't any, just modes of sustainability."

- 2012/07/20 - "It will be sad to lose all these wonderful creatures and landscapes. We all have to do something to protect the planet we live on and the environement. The place where we live is influencing our health and we have to take care of it. I respect the people who founded ...Energy to reduce carbon dioxide emissions and to find alternative energy."

♦ 2010/11/19 – "Yes very informative."

♦ 2010/11/19 – "Any other facts?"

♦ 2013/02/07 – "We can not lose it like this and need to prevent it from happening!"

♦ 2012/05/10 – "Here's a fact for you: orangutans don't live in the Amazon."

♦ 2013/07/24 – "It is everyone's duty to save the world."

♦ 2011/05/12 – "I'm not to sure if this is in here completely or not but, i recently wrote a persuasive essay on this topic. did you know that one in four medicines that are used in the medical feild come from the tropical rainforests? Some examples include the rosy periwincle that contains an anti leukemia drug and the Curare plant is used widely as an anesthetic and to relax muscles for surgery, just to name a few!"

♦ 2017/05/05 – "Sometimes we need to travel to new places to refresh our minds from the city life. I think these are the great places."

♦ 2015/08/25 – "This is a heart touching post that you share with us. I always like these kinds of posts keep it up."

- 2012/06/20 - "This is merely a possible result of every human footprints we left in the earth... Some say this is biological and earthly manner, and they are ripe enough to meet this end."

- 2014/10/24 - "I'm impressed, I must say. Very rarely do I come across a blog that's both informative and entertaining, and let me tell you, you've hit the nail on the head. Your blog is important; the issue is something that not enough people are talking intelligently about."

- 2013/09/30 - "Thanks for sharing the info. Very useful. thanks for sharing this...I was really inspired from you."

- 2015/02/26 - "I found so many interesting stuff in your blog especially its discussion."

- 2014/01/31 - "Reading your content was the best thing I have ever did. Hope to see more of your fresh articles."

- 2015/01/21 - "Amazing style of animals you have seen in this post, I want to say this post is really enjoyable for everyone."

♦ 2014/12/22 – "Great information about animals, I have visited this post I want to say that you have done great sharing."

♦ 2018/04/20 – "Such a outclass blog. I found today providing great information."

♦ 2015/10/30 – "I haven't any word to appreciate this post... Really I am impressed from this post... the person who created this post was a great human...thanks for sharing this with us."

♦ 2016/06/12 – "Absolutely. Amazing sharing."

♦ 2014/12/29 – "Amazing pictures of animals I found here. Some animals are new for me. You have great collection of such animals here. Keep sharing."

♦ 2014/10/27 – "This is my first time I visit here. I discovered such a variety of engrossing stuff in your site, particularly its exchange. From the huge amounts of remarks on your articles, I figure I am by all account not the only one having all the relaxation here! Keep up the astounding work."

♦ 2010/04/12 – "Wow – very informative article. Thank you so much for sharing this."

♦ 2018/07/26 – "Hello, just wanted to say, I loved this article."

- 2013/02/26 - "This is really fantastic and remarkable article. I like the way of your presentation of ideas, views and valuable content. I gained a lot of knowledge from this."
- 2013/12/27 - "It is tempting to comment because of the amazing content on this blog. I wish I had a blog like this."
- 2018/03/21 - "Aw, this was a very good post. Taking a few minutes and actual effort to create a superb article... but what can I say... I procrastinate a whole lot and never seem to get anything done."
- 2015/03/10 - "Amazing! Great post! Wonderful pictures and well written article!"
- 2015/12/30 - "A debt of gratitude is in order for this useful article, sitting tight for articles like this once more."
- 2015/04/07 - "Wow ! Such attractive pictures you did a great job."
- 2018/03/05 - "Nice."
- 2015/03/22 - "Great and soft pictures, my eyes love it!"
- 2015/05/15 - "great images and I love it!"

- 2016/11/30 – "All I can say is to miss few animals not listed."
- 2015/10/22 – "This article was written by a real thinking writer. I agree with many of the solid points made by the writer. I'll be back."
- 2015/11/11 – "Useful information on topics that plenty are interested on for this wonderful post. Admiring the time and effort you put into your blog!"
- 2015/11/22 – "It was a very good post indeed. I thoroughly enjoyed reading it in my lunch time. Will surely come and visit this blog more often. Thanks for sharing."
- 2014/12/09 – "You got a very good website, glad I found it through yahoo."
- 2017/05/11 – "Behind the sunny days, there will be rain and rain, so never lose faith, and keep walking, going to the end of your path."
- 2017/11/23 – "I agree with your post bro. mostly lol"
- 2018/04/20 – "Doing good work. Keep it up."
- 2016/03/15 – "You know such an incredible sum about this subject. Great post!"
- 2018/07/03 – "This article is really fantastic and thanks for sharing the valuable post."

- 2018/10/29 - "Please treat each other well. Everybody has difficulties that we have to overcome, do not know later but how to live each day happily."
- 2018/03/16 - "My brother recommended I might like this website. He was entirely right, I like it very much. This post truly made my day."
- 2018/10/29 - "A very impressive article. I think you have a lot of knowledge about life."
- 2018/03/15 - "THNX :D That's true keep it up."
- 2018/06/12 - "I read this article. I think You put a lot of effort to create this article. I appreciate your work."
- 2018/06/18 - "I can feel that the articles contained in this blog is so interesting. I also get a variety of information, thanks."
- 2018/05/04 - "My friend shared your article because he loves nature and me too. So, I read it then I got know this is a really awesome article about nature. I want to say thank you because you are telling us how we are losing our environment. I hope people understand your beautiful article. I would like to share this then I got know this is really good and people give good feedback."

◆ 2018/01/18 – "Thank for your post! It is easy to understand, detailed and meticulous! I feel it's interesting, your post gave me a new perspective! I have read many other articles about the same topic, but your article convinced me! I hope you continue to have high quality articles like this to share with everyone!"

◆ 2018/06/12 – "If there are many sad stories, share it with the people you trust. Sharing helps people get closer together and you also relieve some of that sadness."

◆ 2018/05/31 – "Your topic is very great and useful for us...thank you."

◆ 2018/05/10 – "This is a wonderful article, Given so much info in it, these types of articles keep the users' interest in the website, and keep on sharing more ... good luck!"

◆ 2018/05/05 – "Really impressive post. I read it whole and going to share it with my social circles. I enjoyed your article and planning to rewrite it on my own blog."

◆ 2018/05/05 – "Thank you, very useful article."

◆ 2018/03/29 – "Excellent info!"

◆ 2018/05/29 – "Very useful info and such good pics."

- 2018/04/27 - "Thank you so much for sharing such superb information with us. Your website is very cool. We are impressed by the details that you have on your site. We Bookmarked this website. Thanks again."
- 2018/01/02 - "Thank you for helping people get the information they need. Great stuff as usual. Keep up the great work!"
- 2017/12/19 - "Are you kidding me ??? I was searching for some good post on this topic last few days and I lost all hope. But see what I found today. Damn good post. Kudos to the writer."
- 2018/04/20 - "I simply couldn't leave your website due to informative content."
- 2017/10/21 - "Touche. Solid arguments. Keep up the great work."
- 2017/09/14 - "I visited your site and after visiting I found that it is very knowledgeable for everyone, you have done really a great job, thank you."
- 2017/08/28 - "I have visited this blog to read something fresh and I really admire you efforts in doing so."

♦ 2015/09/11 – "That is why it is better that you should do relevant research before writing. You will be able to write better post this way."

♦ 2017/06/23 – "I love the new site!! I know how much time, thought, and hard work it takes to bring a new site to fruition. You've done it, and beautifully! I'm raising my glass of tea to you in celebration of this enormous achievement!!! Hopefully, one day I'll have the pleasure to clink glasses with you personally!"

♦ 2017/05/27 – "Fantastic post! Keep up great work."

♦ 2016/12/26 – "Thank you for the information you provide, it helped me a lot! It's great that I know this site! Can you share some updates on how you have made this powerful post!"

♦ 2016/12/05 – "I really hope to see the same high-grade blog posts from you in the future as well."

♦ 2016/09/20 – "I really appreciate this wonderful post that you have provided for us. I just want to let you know that I just check out your site and I find it very interesting and informative. I can't wait to read lots of your posts."

♦ 2016/07/20 – "Thanks for the great post. I liked your writing style most."

- 2015/10/07 – "I really appreciate this wonderful post that you have provided for us. I assure this would be beneficial for most of the people. I am very impressed with it."

- 2016/05/14 – "Awesome blog. I would like to thank you for the efforts you have made in writing this article."

- 2015/11/26 – "I can see that you are an expert at your field! I am launching a website soon, and your information will be very useful for me... Thanks for all your help and wishing you all the success in your business. "

- 2018/05/25 – "I would also be really interested in any pattern you might have seen. Thanks for sharing your insight."

- 2014/08/05 – "The rainforests themselves normally are our protectors, but as the climate gets warmer, instead of absorbing CO_2 to protect our planet's climate, they will be emitting back CO_2 as well. They will be not helping us, the rainforest, if the climate gets warmer. But instead, they will be worsening the global warming problem."

- 2015/03/26 – "This is beautiful post with informative article and enjoyable images."

- 2014/07/21 – "Oh, this article is very interesting. By the way, photos are wonderful. Thanks a lot for it."
- 2013/11/08 – "I am doing something of the same interest and will be taking note on this. Thanks."
- 2013/10/08 – "There are certainly a lot more details to take into consideration, but thanks for sharing this post. I believed it was going to be some boring old article, but it actually compensated for my time. Really great information!!"
- 2013/07/09 – "The article is quite impressive and thoughts put up has clearly got something to state. Nice post!"
- 2013/05/20 – "Really appreciate you sharing this article. Thanks Again. Thanks again for the article post. Really thank you! Much obliged."
- 2014/12/29 – "What a great post shared here. I love this website and happy to find it. I like and appreciated your effort."
- 2013/01/18 – "This is a really good read for me, must admit that you are one of the best bloggers I ever saw. Thanks for posting this informative article."

◆ 2013/01/16 - "Thanks for posting this informative article. I haven't any word to appreciate this post."

◆ 2013/02/25 - "Your article shows you have a lot of background in this topic. Can you direct me to other articles about this? I will recommend this article to my friends as well."

◆ 2013/08/15 - "Your site is good. Actually, I have seen your post and that was very informative and very entertaining for me. Thanks for posting such things. I should recommend your site to my friends. Cheers."

◆ 2013/06/11 - "I have been curious about this topic and decided to do some research. Your article has some useful information. Do you have any more on this subject?"

◆ 2013/07/25 - "I was doing a project and for that I was looking for related information. Some of the points are very useful. Do share some more material if you have."

◆ 2013/05/01 - "It's always nice when you can not only be informed, but also entertained! I'm sure you had fun writing this article. Excellent entry! I'm been looking for topics as interesting as this."

Dean Goodluck

2009/01/29
WCP.Common.Sense

*One touch
of nature*

"One touch of nature
makes the whole world kin."
- William Shakespeare

2009/01/30
WcP.Observer

"SOS Amazon"
Amazon tribes:
"Wake Up, World!"

"SOS Amazon": 1st action of Amazon tribes, sending message "Wake Up, World!" at 2009 World Social Forum in Brazil

www.worldculturepictorial.com/blog/archive/all/2009/01/30

Reader Comments

(not in chronological order)

♦ 2018/02/13 – "1st action of Amazon tribes? Oh my god!"

♦ 2017/12/19 – "This image and Nature look very nice. I will be very happy if I can visit here."

♦ 2017/08/29 – "Nice Amazon information, thanks."

- 2018/12/09 – "This is really very important post for people. Thank you so much for sharing."
- 2018/12/09 – "Your article is awesome! How long does it take to complete this article? I have read through other blogs, but they are cumbersome and confusing. I hope you continue to have such quality articles to share with everyone! I believe there will be many people who share my views when they read this article from you!"
- 2018/03/21 – "I love reading your articles and I shared it with my friends. People also like it and give good feedback. Thank you."
- 2018/03/19 – "Culture define a country. Just love the things."
- 2017/10/30 – "Thanks for sharing this helpful article. Many many thanks."
- 2017/09/22 – "Amazing post."
- 2017/10/17 – "This is really a great article and great read for me. It's my first visit to your blog and i have found it so useful and informative especially this article."

♦ 2017/07/12 - "Thanks for sharing awesome articles, thanks a lot."

♦ 2017/09/17 - "Amazing post! Thanks for sharing."

♦ 2017/03/16 - "Save Amazon. This is exactly what happening in World now."

♦ 2017/03/11 - "Very nice post. Thanks for this."

♦ 2017/09/07 - "Nice post buddy keep it up."

♦ 2013/02/19 - "www.worldculturepictorial.com is terrific. There's often all the appropriate info at the suggestion of my fingers. Thank you and maintain the superior work!"

♦ 2016/04/05 - "This post shares the complete details of the World Social Forum in Brazil at 2009. Actually I got a wonderful opportunity to know the important things in that forum. Keep sharing such posts on this blog!"

Dean Goodluck

2009 / 01 / 31
WCP.Humor

*Half of a house
standing upright
the other half?*

Estranged couple saws house - man moves
half to parents' place, wife lives in
precariously perched, upright half

www.worldculturepictorial.com/ blog/ archive/ all/ 2009/ 01/ 31

2009/02/01
WcP.Observer

Economy in recession
Paris fashion in session

Economy in recession, Paris fashion in session - Haute Couture Fashion Week 2009

www.worldculturepictorial.com/blog/archive/all/2009/02/01

Reader Comments

(not in chronological order)

♦ 2018/11/12 - "Nice design! Wow, I love the pattern and cutting."

♦ 2013/07/15 - "I can't believe how bad things have gotten since the day of this fashion show. The global economy is still yet to improve, which is shocking, especially when you consider how long ago it all started."

♦ 2015/09/23 - "I think economic impact has at one stage shaken fashion industry too, but I agree that most of the things are fine and smooth revenue wise."

♦ 2017/10/31 - "Nice style and great design, this is awesome."

♦ 2015/11/21 - "I like how yakuza looks in Giorgio Armani private section. With the USA style in the right one it shows multiculture style."

♦ 2015/09/15 - "Very nice pictures and dresses."

♦ 2017/08/24 - "Looks very classy design clothes on the model."

♦ 2016/02/10 - "These are the best designs for men. I like the black one the most :)"

♦ 2018/05/13 - "I'm a fashion lover, I feel so happy to found your blog. Thank you for sharing."

♦ 2017/02/07 - "Hi, I like the models of fashion."

♦ 2017/07/13 - "Great to see Haute Couture Fashion Week 2009 pictures, nice."

♦ 2015/12/22 - "Good idea for the design, I like all the design fashion 2016."

♦ 2015/07/30 - "I must admit that you share one of the best information I have read."

♦ 2013/07/22 - "I very much like the clothes, and they are very beautiful!"

- 2011/09/15 - "The John Galliano designs look great. It really shows his knack at making the feminine form sexy and classy at the same time. It is a shame that his most recent incident involving a racist remark and getting fired from Christian Dior would mar his otherwise great career and legacy."

- 2016/02/19 - "I think fashion has been redefined in this post and it could not be better summed up than this. So, we can all say that we feel more and more comfortable following new trends nowadays."

- 2015/12/20 - "Nice website, I like all picture of models."

- 2016/10/09 - "Fantastic. This is excatly fashionable... I love it!!!"

- 2015/07/27 - "Yes you're right. The pictures are very beautiful. And also I was very impressed with the celebration held for fashion. I'm sure it's a fashion photographer who is very reliable because can shoot very well and produce quality fashion photo of outstanding model."

- 2018/11/09 - "The costume design is good and very inspiring, it looks like you are someone who is an expert in this field. Regards."

- 2014/12/10 – "Paris is really the city of fashion."
- 2013/07/15 – "Looked like a really nice fashion show, but who would have known that the situation would have gotten this bad. I guess today, it's time for governments for prioritise, they're even thinking about cutbacks in the movie industry, what next, cutbacks in the computational industry, which would be shocking."
- 2013/06/27 – "Hi, this fashion show is awesome. All the outfits are really beautiful. I really enjoyed this post. Thanks for sharing."
- 2013/10/01 – "Wonderful illustrated information. I thank you about that. No doubt it will be very useful for my future projects."
- 2016/11/26 – "What's up, just wanted to tell you, I liked this post. It was funny. Keep on posting!"
- 2018/12/03 – "Thanks for sharing this amazing article!"
- 2018/11/10 – "Nice costume. Really today I found a nice page and post that you own. Good work and success everything."
- 2018/05/20 – "Thank you for commenting on this website."

- 2018/09/06 - "Thank you brother, your information is very good and friendly, this article is very helpful for me. Thanks for sharing is caring."
- 2018/09/30 - "I feel that it is best to write more on this matter. I like this topic. Thanks."
- 2013/05/14 - "Good post. I learn something new and challenging on blogs I stumbleupon everyday. It's always exciting to read through content from other writers."
- 2018/08/22 - "Very good article! We are linking to this particularly great article on our site. Keep up the good writing."
- 2018/05/23 - "Your post was very nicely written. I'll be back in the future for sure!"
- 2018/05/23 - "Thanks for posting this article. This was just what I was looking for. Keep up good work!"
- 2018/01/22 - "Health is a state of well being of body, soul, and socially to enable more people to live productively socially."
- 2017/09/25 - "I was very impressed by this post, this site has always been pleasant news. Thank you very much for such an interesting post."

- 2017/03/12 – "I simply want to tell you that I am new to weblog and definitely liked this blog site. Very likely I'm going to bookmark your blog. You absolutely have wonderful stories. Cheers for sharing with us your blog."
- 2017/04/06 – "Very rapidly this site will be famous among all blog people, due to its good articles."
- 2017/06/07 – "That's great. Thanks mate for this info."
- 2017/01/14 – "Hello very nice website!!"
- 2016/12/31 – "Must admit that you are among the best bloggers I have read. Thanks for posting this informative article. Very interesting blog. Alot of blogs I see these days don't really provide anything that I'm interested in, but I'm most definately interested in this one. Just thought that I would post and let you know."
- 2016/11/22 – "Very nice and helpful information has been given in this article."
- 2016/05/19 – "Excellent article."
- 2016/07/06 – "I like this post, thank you so much for sharing."
- 2018/05/29 – "Your photos are very nice, I like this site."

- 2016/02/02 - "Feeling happy. Amazing site keep sharing more posts with us..."
- 2015/07/23 - "I like the way you described the topic with such clarity. This is something I have been thinking about for a long time and you really captured the essence of the subject."
- 2016/08/16 - "Your article was excellent and provides great benefits, myself very happy to read it because it can give me more insight, thanks."
- 2016/05/16 - "Found so much interesting stuff in your blog especially its discussion. From the tons of comments on your articles, guess I am not the only one having all the enjoyment here! Keep up the good work."
- 2016/02/05 - "Wonderful blog with precious information. I thank you for sharing this. No doubt it will be very useful for my future projects. Would like to see some of other posts in the near future."
- 2016/10/14 - "Your article was very nice and interesting."
- 2017/06/16 - "I am glad to see your images. Thanks for sharing."

- 2016/05/16 – "Thank you so much for your style fashion show."
- 2015/11/22 – "I love paris, I hope everyone likes this information they shared as I do."
- 2016/05/16 – "Nice design."
- 2015/11/17 – "Wow! This could be one of the most useful blogs we have ever come across on the subject. Actually excellent info! I'm also an expert in this topic so I can understand your effort."
- 2014/12/08 – "This is a good post. This post gives truly quality information."
- 2014/08/23 – "Thank you! Very interesting site."
- 2014/12/08 – "Your article tells me you must have a lot of background in this topic."
- 2014/10/22 – "This is really great job done indeed."
- 2013/12/14 – "I just stumbled upon your blog and wanted to say that I have really enjoyed reading your blog posts. Anyway I'll be subscribing to your feed and I hope you post again soon."
- 2013/12/26 – "Amazing site keep sharing more posts with us..."

- 2014/10/08 - "I was very pleased to discover this website. I want to to thank you for your time just for this wonderful read!! I definitely savored every little bit of it and i also have you saved as a favorite to see new information in your website."

- 2013/12/13 - "A very wonderful article. It touches a lot of urgent issues of our society. We cannot be indifferent to these problems. This article gives good ideas and concepts. Keep it up."

- 2013/07/30 - "I like reading and writing about: 'Haute Couture Fashion'. You have done a great job. I wanted to thank you for this article. I've you bookmarked your internet site to look at out the new stuff you post."

- 2015/11/12 - "I am appreciating it very much! Looking forward to another great article. Good luck to the author! All the best!"

- 2015/02/04 - "Its very humble and noble thing to help our neighbours. After all they are living closer to us then our relatives."

- 2013/05/21 - "Thank you for this interesting article, I did not know this site, will visit you more often."

2009/02/02
System.Thinker

Arctic blizzards
Freezing UK

Arctic blizzards, UK. Freezing snow turns cars, bridges, trees into ice statues. Warm ocean currents 30% less

2009 / 02 / 03
WcP.Art

LuCxeed Photography
Sense and Ideas
on Dais

Dean Goodluck

2009/02/04
WcP.Story.Teller

after 200 years
Founding Father
in tears

Feb. 4, 1789, George Washington was
elected 1st president of America. 1989
Time cover saw Founding Father in tears

www.worldculturepictorial.com/blog/archive/all/2009/02/04

2009/02/05
WcP.System.Thinker

*cook egg on court
at Australia Open*

Once-in-a-century heatwave cripples S AU, buckles rail lines, cooks egg on court at Australia Open in 60C

www.worldculturepictorial.com/blog/archive/all/2009/02/05

Dean Goodluck

2009/02/06
WCP.Story.Teller

1952: what happened?
De Havilland 110

1952: De Havilland 110 had just broken sound barrier when it broke up over spectators showering them with debris

www.worldculturepictorial.com/blog/archive/all/2009/02/06

2009 / 02 / 07
WcP.Poetic.Thought

Every heart sings a song...
another heart whispers back...
At the touch of a lover
everyone becomes a poet

"Every heart sings a song, incomplete,
until another heart whispers back.
Those who wish to sing always find a song.
At the touch of a lover,
everyone becomes a poet."
- Plato

www.worldculturepictorial.com/ blog/ archive/ all/ 2009/ 02/ 07

Dean Goodluck

2009/02/08
WcP.Observer

When will peace drop by?

Turkey's Prime Minister returned home to a hero's welcome for his "courageous stance" against Israel's war in Gaza

www.worldculturepictorial.com/blog/archive/all/2009/02/08

2009/02/09
WcP.Art

Friday January 10th 1964
"The BEATLES Are Coming!"
the kids, the legend
leapt from #43 to #1

Feb 1964, Beatles 1st tour in US; 30 Jan 2009 on London rooftop, Beatles final public concert 40 yrs ago recreated

www.worldculturepictorial.com/ blog/ archive/ all/ 2009/02/09

Reader Comments

◆ 2009/02/11 - "The Beatles are the best band that ever lived! Yes I said it and meant it. John Lennon changes history of the world and led the Beatles to world proportions not achievable until the rise of the Beatles. His messages are still so accurate. Wow, what a concept?"

◆ 2011/03/13 - "Wonderful memories. Since I first heard them when I was about 3, I carry them in my heart. Greatest band! Incredible talent, personality, and charisma. Beatles4Ever!"

Dean Goodluck

2009/02/10
WCP.Poetic.Thought

Pleasure in the pathless woods;
rapture on the lonely shore
By the deep sea,
and music in its roar

"There is pleasure in the pathless woods;
There is rapture on the lonely shore;
There is society, where none intrudes,
By the deep sea, and music in its roar:
I love not man the less, but Nature more."
- Lord Byron

www.worldculturepictorial.com/blog/archive/all/2009/02/10

Reader Comments

♦ 2015/11/03 – "This is a topic that is close to my heart... Take care! Where are your contact details though?"

2009 / 02 / 11
WcP.Story.Teller

newest republic
and century-old culture

World's newest republic maintains a unique century-old culture - Nepalese girl, 3, begins life as "living goddess"

www.worldculturepictorial.com / blog / archive / all / 2009 / 02 / 11

Reader Comments

◆ 2015/11/03 - "Culture is different in countries and people from all over the world make use of such according to specified matter. There are many people who celebrate much function in their country and their people make necessary preparation."

◆ 2018/10/16 - "Very nice post."

2009/02/12
WcP.Observer

Photo: grandpa in 80s with 9-year-old granddaughter

08Feb2009 Photo. Family without a home. Sayed Abdul Karim, 80, sits with 9-yr-old granddaughter, Camina, in a camp

www.worldculturepictorial.com/blog/archive/all/2009/02/12

2009/02/13
WcP.Scientific.Mind

Ocean Mysteries:
jellyfish reverting to younger self

Ocean Mysteries: 'Immortal' jellyfish from Caribbean capable of reverting to younger self spreading all over world

www.worldculturepictorial.com/blog/archive/all/2009/02/13

Dean Goodluck

2009/02/14
WCP.Humor

Nature's Wonder
Valentine's Day
Ox born with
heart-shaped birthmark

Nature's Wonder. Ox born ahead of Valentine's Day with heart-shaped birthmark, faithful geese couple, baby zebra & mother

www.worldculturepictorial.com/blog/archive/all/2009/02/14

2009/02/15
WcP.Watchful.Eye

Earth orbit
Man-made junk jam

Man-made junk in low Earth orbit: satellite collision highlights space pollution and rising hazard from debris

www.worldculturepictorial.com/ blog/ archive/ all/ 2009/02/15

Dean GoodLuck

2009 /02 /16
WCP.Philosophy

Einstein on
Science and religion

"Science without religion is lame,
religion without science is blind."
- Albert Einstein

www.worldculturepictorial.com/ blog/ archive/ all/ 2009/ 02/ 16

2009/02/17
WcP.Humor

Jokes
Alabaman headlines
Alaska nights

50 Jokes for 50 US States (part i): Alabaman headlines, Alaska nights, catching rabbits in California, and more...

www.worldculturepictorial.com/blog/archive/all/2009/02/17

Reader Comments

◆ 2014/10/27 – "Hi I'm so excited I found your site, I really found you by mistake while searching on Askjeeve for something else, regardless I'm here now and would just like to say thanks a lot for a fantastic post and an all round thrilling blog (I also love the theme/design). When I have time I will be back to read much more. Please do keep up the awesome work."

2009/02/18
WCP.Tomorrows.History

1st Emperor of United China QinShiHuang (18Feb259–10Sep210 BC)

1st Emperor of United China, QinShiHuang (18Feb259–10Sep210 BC) standardized measurement, currency, Chinese script, built Great Wall

www.worldculturepictorial.com/blog/archive/all/2009/02/18

2009/02/19
WcP.Story.Teller

retired 747 jet
mighty bird 'Jumbo Hostel'

Imagination? Nope. World's 1st aircraft, retired 747 jet, converted into hotel: mighty bird "Jumbo Hostel"

www.worldculturepictorial.com/blog/archive/all/2009/02/19

Dean Goodluck

2009/02/20
WCP.Story.Teller

Rescue flight
birds follow
ultralight plane

Rescue flight in blue sky. Guiding young
whooping cranes to winter nesting
grounds: birds follow ultralight plane

www.worldculturepictorial.com/blog/archive/all/2009/02/20

150

2009 / 02 / 21
WcP.Life.Coach

Nature's broadcasting
will you tune in?

"I love to think of nature as
an unlimited broadcasting station,
through which God speaks to us every hour,
if we will only tune in."
- George Washington Carver

www.worldculturepictorial.com/blog/archive/all/2009/02/21

Dean Goodluck

2009 / 02 / 22
WCP.Observer

Bolivia's first indigenous President

Bolivia's first indigenous President enacts new constitution, empowers indigenous majority, allows for land reform

www.worldculturepictorial.com/ blog/ archive/ all/ 2009/ 02/ 22

2009 / 02 / 23
WcP.Movie.Critic

Song & dance
81st annual Academy Awards

Song & dance, euphoria & sobriety, and a few moving moments at the 81st annual Academy Awards

www.worldculturepictorial.com/ blog/ archive/ all/ 2009/ 02/ 23

Reader Comments

◆ 2016/05/03 - "Firstly, I congratulate the team of Slumdog Millionaire movie. I always saw the latest updates about movies and award news. Its really great success for our Indian cinemas that the Bollywood movie was nominated for the Oscar awards. Every Indian should glad to hear this news. This news makes us feel proud."

2009/02/24
WCP.Scientific.Mind

Science of Snowflakes
Simple, complex

Snowflakes are science and art: see ice crystals, simple, complex, the basics behind these miniature miracles of Nature

www.worldculturepictorial.com/blog/archive/all/2009/02/24

Reader Comments

◆ 2016/04/27 – "Hey there, You have done a fantastic job. I'll definitely digg it and personally suggest to my friends. I am confident they will benefit from this web site."

2009/02/25
WcP.Story.Teller

Photo
Brazilian Amazon
woman and naked child vs armor

Heavy Heart. 11Mar08 photo. Brazilian Amazon: woman holds naked child, being pushed away from her home by heavily armed

www.worldculturepictorial.com/blog/archive/all/2009/02/25

Dean Goodluck

2009/02/26
WcP.Observer

Chile
Karukinka Nature Reserve

Wildlife Conservation Society and Goldman Sachs safeguard Chile's Karukinka Nature Reserve, home to 700 plant species and more

www.worldculturepictorial.com/blog/archive/all/2009/02/26

2009/02/27
WcP.Observer

final Sherlock Holmes novel
by Sir Arthur Conan Doyle

2 7 Feb 1915 The Valley of Fear 4th and final Sherlock Holmes novel by Arthur Conan Doyle published

www.worldculturepictorial.com/blog/archive/all/2009/02/27

2009/02/28
WCP.Tomorrows.History

idealist believes the short run
cynic believes the long run
realist?

"An idealist believes the short run doesn't count.
A cynic believes the long run
doesn't matter.
A realist believes that what is done
or left undone in the short run
determines the long run."
- Sydney J. Harris

www.worldculturepictorial.com/blog/archive/all/2009/02/28

2009/03/01
WcP.Story.Teller

tallest buildings
Taipei Tower 101
Burj Dubai & 1-km High Club

World's tallest buildings (part iii): Taipei Tower 101, Burj Dubai & 1-km High Club (projects under construction)

www.worldculturepictorial.com/blog/archive/all/2009/03/01

Reader Comments

♦ 2016/01/14 – "I wonder how it could be possible, such massive giant structure, I just wanna appreciate the planning of the architects and engineers who have built those tallest towers. I am amazed to see this comparison with other towers."

♦ 2015/12/09 - "Taipei tower is one of the most beautiful buildings over the country. Such towers can't be stood by any ordinary architect but all the measurements need to be done well for the building to stand. Behind the construction companies, technology is the one that plays the vital role. Only construction companies can never make such mega-structures but they need help of IT services. At present we can find lots of such infra-structures all over the world and with coming days there are more inventions to look forward to."

♦ 2017/08/23 - "The Goldin Finance 117 tower is a 597-metre-high skyscraper designed by the P&T Group. Located in Tianjin, China, this diamond-shaped building will be completed in 2016 and it will house offices and a hotel. The Goldin Finance 117 just measures 2 meters less than the Ping An Financial Centre, so it achieves position 5 in the list of the world's tallest buildings."

♦ 2016/10/21 - "Sao Paulo has one of the the world's worst daily traffic jams. Great care and attention is required when driving in Sao Paulo."

◆ 2012/02/27 - "Engineers really need to think outside the box in order to maintain the day to day functions of everyday affairs like plumbing and flushing because the height causes all sorts of problems. I think if the windows were open at the top, the winds would cause doors to slam so hard they might just break apart. I wonder how high can engineers continue to build these buildings before they hit a limit."

◆ 2012/11/05 - "History has shown no limitation stops man, so if engineers decide to build higher skyscraper, they surely would solve such problems."

◆ 2017/04/24 - "Amazing info! And beautiful buildings."

◆ 2014/06/24 - "Both of these buildings, the Taipei tower and the Burj Khalifa are the most admirable buildings ever built. I have been to Burj Khalifa once, and the view from one of the top floors is simple awesome. Thanks for sharing."

◆ 2012/06/20 - "I think at this point in time no one beats the Burj Dubai for being the tallest skyscrapers building in the world."

- 2013/11/15 - "A lot of new building were built in the last few years, the Burj Dubai building is gorgeous and will keep its title as the tallest building in the world for a lot of years. I am interested about the construction of new buildings. The new plans for the Al Burj building look great, a 1200 m building needs to be constructed using the latest technologies."

- 2013/04/29 - "I have always been passionate about architecture and travel as well and I have seen most of the tallest buildings in the world but sadly, I never went to Dubai or see the Taipei tower. I am currently visiting France and I am planning on taking a trip to the United Arab Emirates. I have heard a lot of things about the architectural wonders in Dubai and I want to get the chance to see them with my own eyes. It will certainly be a vacation I will never forget."

- 2017/12/14 - "I didn't know Dubai have the tallest building in the world."

- 2014/03/20 - "Burj Dubai is really awesome."

- 2017/08/02 - "This was truly a fascinating theme and I kinda concur with what you have said here!"

♦ 2017/03/29 - "Your blog is very knowledgeable and good."

♦ 2017/10/21 - "I like it. This cultural aspect is really something to look into."

♦ 2017/08/11 - "This is a savvy blog. I would not joke about this. You have such a great amount of learning about this issue, thus much energy. You additionally know how to make individuals rally behind it, clearly from the reactions."

♦ 2017/09/25 - "They could have done better."

♦ 2018/04/20 - "The article you have shared here very awesome. I really like and appreciate your work. I read deeply your article, the points you have mentioned in this article are useful."

♦ 2017/11/30 - "So beautiful. I enjoy the subject you are talking about. It very interesting! Thanks for sharing!"

♦ 2017/09/21 - "Thank you. Your blog has nice information, I have good ideas from this amazing blog."

♦ 2017/09/20 - "Very good, I think I found the knowledge I needed. I will see and refer some information in your post. thank you."

- 2016/07/27 - "High and Higher... Thank you! I've found what I need. I constantly wanted to write on my site something like that. Could I may have this post to my site?"
- 2017/09/18 - "You have done a great job on this article. It's very readable and highly intelligent. You have even managed to make it understandable and easy to read. You have some real writing talent. Thank you. "
- 2017/08/07 - "Thank you for your work on the blog! You're doing a good job!"
- 2017/06/27 - "I loved it.Thank you for the information you shared."
- 2018/08/08 - "This article gives the light in which we can watch the truth. This is exceptionally decent one and gives in-depth data. A debt of gratitude is in order for this decent article."
- 2017/07/29 - "Fabulous... Astounding... I'll bookmark your online journal... I'm cheerful to discover such helpful information here in the post, much obliged for sharing."
- 2016/07/22 - "I really like the dear information you offer in your articles."

♦ 2017/07/28 - "Wow I can say that this is another great article as expected of this blog. Bookmarked this site.."

♦ 2017/08/06 - "Positive webpage, where did you think of the data on this posting? I have perused a couple of the articles on your site now, and I truly like your style. Much obliged and please keep up the powerful work."

♦ 2016/01/06 - "Your blog was too good. I really appreciate your blog. Thanks for sharing."

♦ 2016/03/31 - "Great article. Keep uploading."

♦ 2017/07/27 - "You have a real ability for writing unique content. I like how you think and the way you represent your views in this article. I agree with your way of thinking. Thank you for sharing."

♦ 2016/03/24 - "I like this post very much, thanks."

♦ 2015/09/15 - "Really impressive post. I read it whole and going to share it with my social circles. I enjoyed your article and planning to rewrite it on my own blog."

- 2017/08/06 - "Sublimely composed article, if just all bloggers offered the same substance as you, the web would be an obviously better place..."
- 2016/06/08 - "These are genuinely enormous ideas concerning blogging. You have touched some nice factors here. Anyway keep up writing."
- 2017/11/27 - "Quite great put up. I simply stumbled upon your blog and desired to mention that I have truely enjoyed surfing your weblog posts. In any case I'll be subscribing to your feed and I hope you write again soon!"
- 2017/10/09 - "This is one of the best articles I've ever read, thanks for sharing."

2009/03/02
WcP.Movie.Critic

Children's Film Festival
100 films from
30 countries

More than just child's play at New York
International Children's Film Festival:
movies where kids call the shots

www.worldculturepictorial.com/blog/archive/all/2009/03/02

Dean Goodluck

2009/03/03
WCP.Story.Teller

How come?
200 whales and dolphins
get stranded together

Australian wildlife rescuers and 100+ island volunteers race to save 200 stranded whales and dolphins off Tasmania

www.worldculturepictorial.com/blog/archive/all/2009/03/03

Reader Comments

♦ 2016/04/07 – "Author actually chooses very complex topic and narrates it to very simple and easy words."

♦ 2009/03/18 – "I recently came across your blog and have been reading along. I thought I would leave my first comment. I don't know what to say except that I have enjoyed reading. Nice blog. I will keep visiting this blog very often."

2009/03/04
WcP.Story.Teller

Sea gypsies
houses on stilts
no electricity

Sea gypsies: the Samah who live in the Sulawesi Sea off Malaysia's state of Sabah

www.worldculturepictorial.com/blog/archive/all/2009/03/04

Dean Goodluck

2009/03/04
WCP.Scientific.Mind

MIT
sleek solar 90-mph car
to take World Solar Challenge

MIT Solar Electric Vehicle Team unveils sleek 90-mph car, will compete in World Solar Challenge in Australia

www.worldculturepictorial.com/blog/archive/all/2009/03/04

Reader Comments

♦ 2016/03/23 – "The whole new solar car Eleanor is very much efficient in its running condition as well as its appearance. I truly appreciate the whole team who have designed this car."

♦ 2017/03/04 – "Now that design is on another level, it is very nice, very creative."

- 2017/02/08 - "MIT students are really talented. How do you build such a breathtaking gadget."
- 2012/03/02 - "Best of luck. The MIT team has always been very innovative and I look forward to seeing more of their designs at these challenges."
- 2012/08/29 - "The current designs of solar cars are still mostly wide and flat. I understand that the engineers need to work under the limitations of today's technology, but is there anyway to make a solar car more pleasing to the eye? Kudos to them for setting a good speed, but I think aesthetics need to be considered too."
- 2017/02/20 - "The design is very classic. It displays a lot of creativity."
- 2012/03/15 - "I believe such competitions display the abilities of the solar powered electrical vehicle, in terms of speed and efficiency. Though the designs here are for competition purposes, some elements can be used for street cars, and someday we might see solar powered vehicles all over the world."

- 2012/03/20 - "Awesome car. I think this is the first solar car that runs like this? 90mph? That is very impressive considering the other solar cars. You think that this car is the solution on the ever changing auto industry?"
- 2012/05/01 - "This is very interesting. The solar power represents the future. I heared about it at an event and everybody was so captivated."
- 2011/06/27 - "Great car. This car was built for one purpose, to race in Australia! That's it!!"
- 2012/07/19 - "I know a little bit. Solar cars combine technology typically used in the aerospace, bicycle, alternative energy and automotive industries. The design of a solar vehicle is severely limited by the energy input into the car (batteries and power from the sun). Virtually all solar cars ever built have been for the purpose of solar car races (with notable exceptions)."

♦ 2012/11/04 - "Yes, you are right. It's based on the mechanism of spaceships. I mean in spaceship, solar energy is also used. But I'm suspicious about the overall effectiveness of this car as would it be able to get energy at a cloudy day? Probably it's also not totally solar energy based car."

♦ 2012/04/13 - "The design is very futuristic. Maybe in the future we'll have to give away our old cars and buy this one and we'll get rid of headache caused by searching different auto parts."

♦ 2017/02/20 - "I agree with you, the design still looks good."

2009/03/05
WcP.Poetic.Thought

So We'll Go
No More A-Roving
Poem by Lord Byron

So we'll go no more a-roving
So late into the night,
Though the heart still be as loving,
And the moon still be as bright.

For the sword outwears its sheath,
And the soul outwears the breast,
And the heart must pause to breathe,
And love itself have rest.

Though the night was made for loving,
And the day returns too soon,
Yet we'll go no more a-roving
By the light of the moon.

So We'll Go No More A-Roving
- by Lord Byron

2009/03/06
WcP.Art

Photography
Kenya
Elephants

African Elephants dwarfed by acacias in Kenya - photo from 2009 Sony World Photography Awards

www.worldculturepictorial.com/blog/archive/all/2009/03/06

Reader Comments

♦ 2009/03/13 - "This is a great picture! I love the way the clouds look in the skies, and the acacia trees put in perspective. Your eyes need one or two seconds to find the elephants, and then it's magic! I was in Kenya last year and took a similar picture."

♦ 2010/12/17 - "Check out these interesting African Elephant Facts and learn more about the biggest land mammal in the world. Elephants are unique animals that live in parts of the Africa. There are two types of elephants, the Asian elephant and the African elephant. African Elephant is split into two species, the African Forest Elephant and the African Bush Elephant. Elephants are the largest land living mammal in the world. Both the female and the male African elephants have tusks but only the male Asian elephants have tusks. They use their tusks for digging and finding food."

♦ 2017/07/23 - "Wow that was a good picture looking very beautiful with wild elephants strolling in the forest. I would like to appreciate the photographer for his hard work and his dedication in taking this picture this beautifully. I want to request photographer to share this picture in a blog and try creating a blog page to post more of these kinds of pictures."

2009 / 03 / 07
WcP.Scientific.Mind

NASA
looking for
Earth's twin

NASA's spacecraft Kepler blasts off on a three-year mission in search of Earth-like planets

www.worldculturepictorial.com / blog / archive / all / 2009 / 03 / 07

Dean Goodluck

2009/03/08
WCP.Philosophy

Einstein
on
the mysterious

"The most beautiful experience
we can have is the mysterious...
the fundamental emotion which stands
at the cradle of true art and true science."
- Albert Einstein

www.worldculturepictorial.com/blog/archive/all/2009/03/08

2009 / 03 / 09
WcP.Story.Teller

screaming "God, she fell in!"
he jumped down to the tracks
light coming into the tunnel

Hero in Our Life: with seconds from an oncoming train, one man risked everything to save a woman he'd never met

www.worldculturepictorial.com / blog / archive / all / 2009 / 03 / 09

Dean Goodluck

2009/03/10
WCP.Scientific.Mind

1969
20th-century engineering
supersonic Concorde

On Mar 2, 1969 world's first supersonic jetliner Concorde took flight, feat of collaboration engineering and work of beauty

www.worldculturepictorial.com/blog/archive/all/2009/03/10

2009/03/11
WcP.Story.Teller

luxury cars in
worst recession
since World War II

Protesters in Berlin rage at economic
plight by torching expensive cars -
symbols of German wealth and power

www.worldculturepictorial.com/ blog/ archive/ all/ 2009/03/11

Dean Goodluck

2009/03/12
WCP.Story.Teller

Very moving photo
boy at 3
saying goodbye
to his dad

3-year-old little boy bows head to his father in line with soldiers deployed as part of Massachusetts National Guard

www.worldculturepictorial.com/blog/archive/all/2009/03/12

Reader Comments

◆ 2009/03/13 – "Wow! That's a very cute picture!"

◆ 2009/05/25 – "Very moving photo."

- 2016/03/03 – "Oh no this is such a sad thing which I have noticed the little kid in this picture. He stood by his father with a sad face. Extremely heartfelt. So sad, saying goodbye to his dad is such a painful thing."

- 2016/03/23 – "Owwww, touching... Feel so sad, he loves his father..."

- 2018/09/23 – "Amazing!!! Good work. Keep it up. Thanks given."

Dean Goodluck

2009 / 03 / 13
WCP.Observer

Shoe steps
into politics

Shoe has position in politics? Never before
as it does now. Iraqis divided over jail
sentence for shoe thrower

www.worldculturepictorial.com/blog/archive/all/2009/03/13

2009/03/14
WcP.System.Thinker

Einstein at 4
on a pocket compass
"something behind things"

130 years ago today: March 14, 1879, Birth of Albert Einstein - Emblem of Reason, Icon of Wisdom

www.worldculturepictorial.com/blog/archive/all/2009/03/14

Dean Goodluck

2009/03/15
WCP.Watchful.Eye

"loopholes"

Taxes' many faces: hard times mean a hard look at taxes - how much we pay, who skates through loopholes and more

www.worldculturepictorial.com/blog/archive/all/2009/03/15

2009/03/16
WcP.Observer

Pope Benedict XVI
unusual step

Vatican's rare step: Pope Benedict XVI admits errors, takes frank look at controversy over Holocaust-denying bishop

www.worldculturepictorial.com/blog/archive/all/2009/03/16

Dean Goodluck

2009/03/17
WcP.Observer

coffins in a village

In main town of Pakistan's tribal area along Afghanistan border, death toll rises. Pakistan urges Obama to halt missile attacks

www.worldculturepictorial.com/blog/archive/all/2009/03/17

2009/03/18
WcP.System.Thinker

1st International Polar Year proposed by an Austro-Hungarian naval officer in 1875

March 18, 2009. Canada marks "Oceans and Marine Life Polar Day", International Polar Year (the 1st IPY: 1882–1883) webcast event

www.worldculturepictorial.com/blog/archive/all/2009/03/18

Dean Goodluck

2009/03/19
WcP.Art

tea plantation
boundless green

Tea plantation: Earth must feel profound peace, and enjoy its fresh breaths amidst vast green. Who wouldn't?

www.worldculturepictorial.com/blog/archive/all/2009/03/19

2009/03/20
WcP.System.Thinker

crisis in Europe

Financial crisis deprives livelihood.
Poverty sparks fury, raging across Europe:
Iceland, France, Russia, Greece...

www.worldculturepictorial.com/blog/archive/all/2009/03/20

2009/03/21
WCP.Philosophy

Conscience is God
present in man

"Conscience is God present in man."
- Victor Hugo

www.worldculturepictorial.com/blog/archive/all/2009/03/21

2009/03/22
WcP.Watchful.Eye

He looks out over tent city
as storm clouds gather above

"Great Depression had Hoovervilles. 70's crisis snaking gas lines. Today's recession is about disappearing wealth"

www.worldculturepictorial.com/blog/archive/all/2009/03/22

Reader Comments

♦ 2009/03/24 - "Actually - We have Bushvilles."

2009/03/23
WCP.Poetic.Thought

Her early leaf's a flower;
But only so an hour

"Nature's first green is gold
Her hardest hue to hold.
Her early leaf's a flower;
But only so an hour.
Then leaf subsides to leaf.
So Eden sank to grief,
So dawn goes down to day.
Nothing gold can stay."

- Robert Frost

www.worldculturepictorial.com/blog/archive/all/2009/03/23

2009/03/24
WcP.Observer

Africa's youngest president
an entrepreneur
a charismatic disc jockey

Africa: a charismatic disc jockey, 34-year-old fresh-faced entrepreneur is sworn in as Africa's youngest president

www.worldculturepictorial.com/blog/archive/all/2009/03/24

Dean Goodluck

2009/03/25
WcP.System.Thinker

Melting glaciers
shrinking borders
4,000 meters above sea level

Melting glaciers in Europe force Italy and Switzerland to officially redraw their borders

www.worldculturepictorial.com/blog/archive/all/2009/03/25

2009 / 03 / 26
WcP.Story.Teller

first prize
of World Press Photo Contest
cloud of debris soared
high into air

What's woken up Chaiten volcano in Chile dormant for thousands of years suddenly erupted? 2008 spectacular photo

www.worldculturepictorial.com/ blog/ archive/ all/ 2009/ 03/ 26

197

Dean Goodluck

2009/03/27
WCP.Story.Teller

Floating treasure
tempting sea
piracy of modern age

Floating treasure, tempting sea. World's biggest ship hijacking by pirates off coast of Somalia for $3 million ransom

www.worldculturepictorial.com/blog/archive/all/2009/03/27

Reader Comments

♦ 2018/04/10 - "This is not good news for us, very miserable conditions there. When I heard this news, I am very worried. I think people stand against this problem and take some good step and solve this problem. Please share all the details here."

2009/03/28
WcP.Publisher

dim
time zone by time zone

Earth Hour: time zone by time zone,
~4000 cities and towns in 88 countries
dim nonessential lights from 8:30-9:30pm

www.worldculturepictorial.com/blog/archive/all/2009/03/28

Dean Goodluck

2009/03/29
WCP.Philosophy

Thinking:
The talking of the soul with itself

"Thinking:
The talking of the soul with itself."
- Plato

www.worldculturepictorial.com/blog/archive/all/2009/03/29

2009 / 03 / 30
WcP.Observer

Polar bears
vs
submarine

Uneasy polar bears watching submarine emerging out of broken icy snow. Arctic losing ice, **giving huge noise**

www.worldculturepictorial.com / blog / archive / all / 2009 / 03 / 29

Reader Comments

◆ 2009/04/02 – "It's sad to see the ice melt so fast. Those poor animals have no other habitat. I hope we can fix this soon."

Dean Goodluck

2009 / 03 / 31
WcP.Observer

After 6 years
British getting smarter

Smart! All 4100 British troops will be out of violence-wracked Iraq by end of July after years' invasion

www.worldculturepictorial.com / blog / archive / all / 2009 / 03 / 31

2009/04/02
WcP.System.Thinker

circling
Arctic circle

Earth's pole, now less ice but disturbed peace: Canada, Denmark, Norway, Russia, US all claim a piece of Arctic circle

www.worldculturepictorial.com/blog/archive/all/2009/04/02

Dean Goodluck

2009 / 04 / 04
WCP.Story.Teller

Lincoln's
prophetic dream

April 4 - President Abraham Lincoln's prophetic dream about assassination that happened 10 days later

www.worldculturepictorial.com / blog / archive / all / 2009 / 04 / 04

2009 / 04 / 06
WcP.Common.Sense

*Australian banks
against tides*

Leadership: when many governments busy bailing out big business, Australian banks to give mortgage help to jobless

www.worldculturepictorial.com / blog / archive / all / 2009 / 04 / 06

Dean Goodluck

2009 / 04 / 07
WCP.Common.Sense

Australia getting smart
pulling out too

Courage! Australian PM Kevin Rudd admits going to war with Iraq was wrong, pulling all AU troops back home

www.worldculturepictorial.com/blog/archive/all/2009/04/07

2009/04/09
WcP.Poetic.Thought

Poem
by Robert Frost
Love and A Question

A stranger came to the door at eve,
And he spoke the bridegroom fair.
He bore a green-white stick in his hand,
And, for all burden, care.
He asked with the eyes more than the lips
For a shelter for the night,
And he turned and looked at the road afar
Without a window light.

- from Love And A Question
by Robert Frost

www.worldculturepictorial.com/ blog/ archive/ all/ 2009/04/09

Dean Goodluck

2009/04/11
WCP.System.Thinker

loss of polar ice
shift axis of Earth?

Antarctic ice shelves (some intact for 10,000 yrs) loss may shift axis of Earth. Wilkins Ice Shelf diminished by 30%

www.worldculturepictorial.com/blog/archive/all/2009/04/11

2009/04/12
WcP.Common.Sense

Capt. Richard Phillips of hijacked US-flagged Danish-owned freighter Maersk Alabama

Hail to hero! Captain who saved 19-crew's lives when US-flagged, Danish-owned freighter hijacked by pirates

www.worldculturepictorial.com/blog/archive/all/2009/04/12

Dean Goodluck

2009/04/13
WCP.Story.Teller

Thomas Jefferson
first Secretary of State
in 1790-1793
under President George Washington

Thomas Jefferson (April 13, 1743 – July 4, 1826), principal author of Declaration of Independence, and 3rd President of United States from 1801 to 1809

www.worldculturepictorial.com/blog/archive/all/2009/04/13

2009/04/15
WcP.Story.Teller

not an easy job

Disturbing: War thirsts for blood. Soldiers in demand. Pressure on recruiters: 17 died by their own hand since '01

www.worldculturepictorial.com/blog/archive/all/2009/04/15

Dean Goodluck

2009/04/17
WCP.Scientific.Mind

orbiting solar farm in space
Satellite solar cells

Satellite solar panels in orbit to capture sun's rays 24/7 and wirelessly beam energy down to Earth

www.worldculturepictorial.com/blog/archive/all/2009/04/17

2009/04/19
WcP.Humor

*May you live
every day of your life*

"May you live every day of your life."
- Jonathan Swift

www.worldculturepictorial.com / blog / archive / all / 2009 / 04 / 19

2009/04/20
WCP.Tomorrows.History

Paris, France
April 20, 1887
World's First Motor Race

April 20, 1887. Bouton and his co-driver won World's First Motor Race (on a steam-powered quadricycle), Paris, France

www.worldculturepictorial.com/blog/archive/all/2009/04/20

2009/04/21
WcP.Observer

France
Time to be at peace with itself

Conscience: Time to be at peace with itself, France to compensate victims sickened by nuclear tests

www.worldculturepictorial.com/blog/archive/all/2009/04/21

2009/04/22
WCP.Tomorrows.History

Netherlands
first heavy traffic wooden bridge
Spanning 105 feet

Earth must be amazed to see world's first heavy traffic road bridge made of Wood, Gift from Earth!

www.worldculturepictorial.com/blog/archive/all/2009/04/22

Reader Comments

◆ 2009/04/22 – "You've got to see this wooden bridge. Beautiful and creative."

♦ 2010/02/24 - "Congratulations but you're not the first or the longest

I've built wood bridges that were designed to carry a lot heavier loads here in British Columbia Canada and a quick search found that the US Forest Service has many wood bridges that can carry 102 ton logging trucks (U102) and 90 ton log loaders (L90). The longest clear span I've heard of so far was 121 ft.

I congratulate the City of Sneek for using wood and encourage more of it but the jury is still out one who had the first, who has the longest and whose can carry the most."

♦ 2013/09/12 - "Impressive work and design! Never thought that I could see a bridge that is made of wood yet I can see its strength to handle it but how long it would take? Will it also last for decades as the steel bridges perform?"

Dean Goodluck

2009/04/23
WCP.Poetic.Thought

William Shakespeare
Born: April 23, 1564
Died: April 23, 1616 (aged 52)

Timeless. Shakespeare wrote 38 plays, 154 sonnets and many poems. His plays have been translated into every major living language and performed more often than any other playwright

www.worldculturepictorial.com/blog/archive/all/2009/04/23

2009 / 04 / 25
WcP.Humor

folks keeping their spirits up
Jobless compete
at unemployment Olympics

First ever Jobless Olympics: upbeat mood,
free time granted, contestants have fun
and winners stand on carbon boxes

www.worldculturepictorial.com/ blog/ archive/ all/ 2009/ 04/ 25

2009/04/27
WcP.Poetic.Thought

"Mutual fear brings Peace,
Till selfish loves increase;
Then Cruelty knits a snare,
And spreads his baits with care"

Pity would be no more
If we did not make somebody poor,
And Mercy no more could be
If all were as happy as we.

And mutual fear brings Peace,
Till the selfish loves increase;
Then Cruelty knits a snare,
And spreads his baits with care.

He sits down with holy fears,
And waters the ground with tears;
Then Humility takes its root
Underneath his foot.

Soon spreads the dismal shade
Of Mystery over his head,
And the caterpillar and fly
Feed on the Mystery.

And it bears the fruit of Deceit,
Ruddy and sweet to eat,
And the raven his nest has made
In its thickest shade.

The gods of the earth and sea
Sought through nature to find this tree,
But their search was all in vain:
There grows one in the human Brain.

- The Human Abstract
by William Blake

www.worldculturepictorial.com/blog/archive/all/2009/04/27

Dean Goodluck

2009/04/29
WCP.System.Thinker

Masked horseman
Masked kiss for lovers

Nature fed up with animals being ill-confined, force-fed? First cows mad, then bird flu, now deadly virus from swine

www.worldculturepictorial.com/blog/archive/all/2009/04/29

Reader Comments

♦ 2009/04/29 – "Check out this cartoon about Spider Pig and swine flu!"

2009/04/30
WcP.Life.Coach

*I still find each day too short for
all the thoughts I want to think,
all the walks I want to take...*

"I still find each day too short
for all the thoughts I want to think,
all the walks I want to take,
all the books I want to read
and all the friends I want to see."
- John Burroughs

www.worldculturepictorial.com/blog/archive/all/2009/04/30

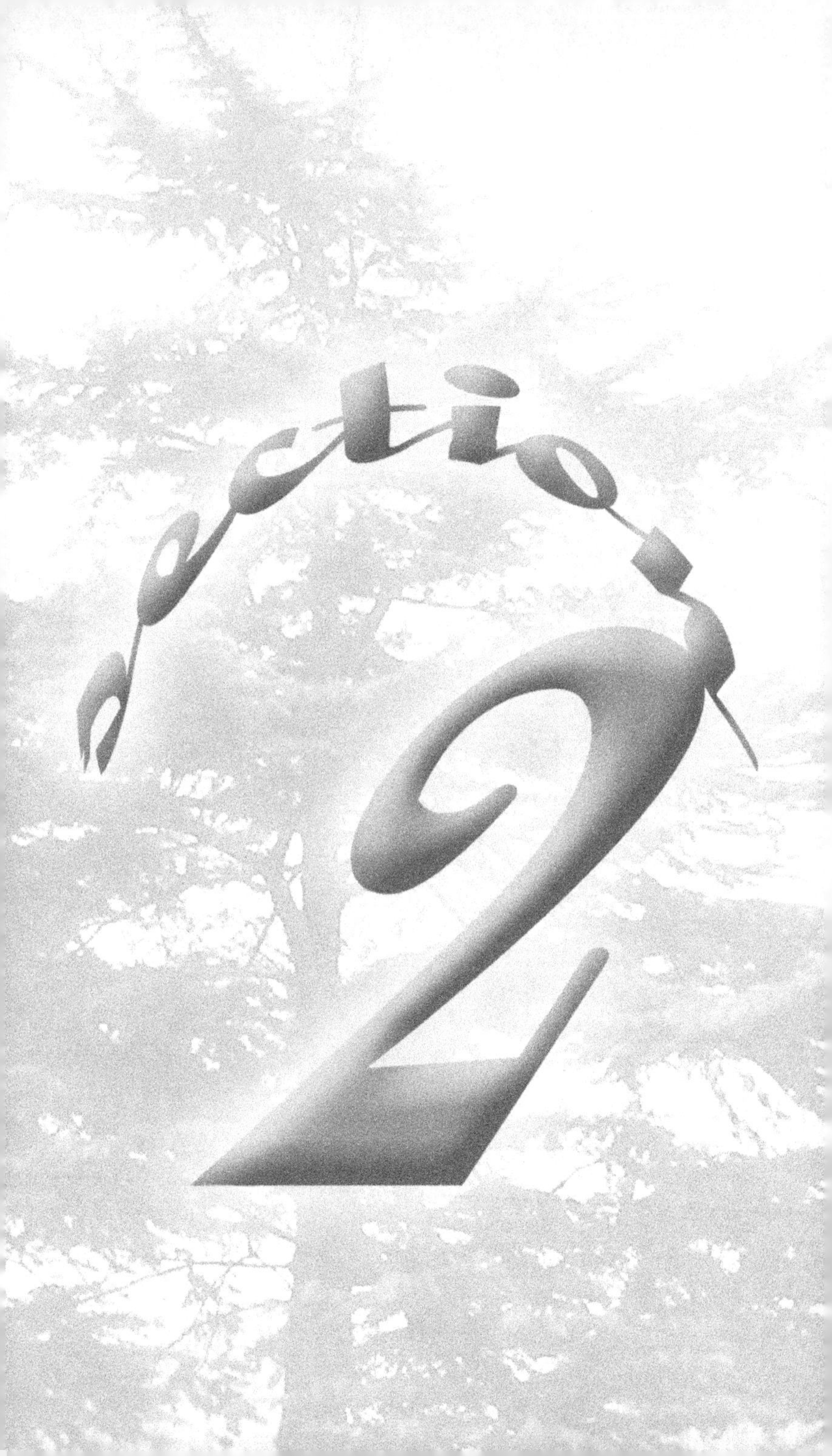
section
2

...nic Stevenson

"Wine is
bottled
poetry"

Grape holds Wine, Poetry Philosophy.

Dean Goodluck

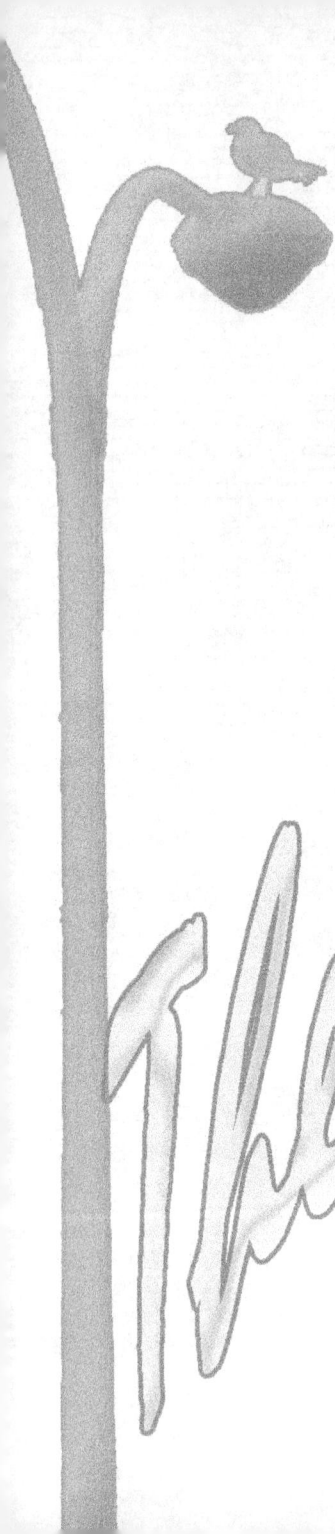

The Will

228

Poem
The Will
John Donne

Before I sigh my last gasp, let me breathe,
Great Love, some legacies ; I here bequeath
Mine eyes to Argus, if mine eyes can see ;
If they be blind, then, Love, I give them thee ;
My tongue to Fame ; to ambassadors mine ears ;
To women, or the sea, my tears ;
Thou, Love, hast taught me heretofore
By making me serve her who had twenty more,
That I should give to none,
    but such as had too much before.

My constancy I to the planets give ;
My truth to them who at the court do live ;
My ingenuity and openness,
To Jesuits ; to buffoons my pensiveness ;
My silence to any, who abroad hath been ;
My money to a Capuchin :
Thou, Love, taught'st me, by appointing me
To love there, where no love received can be,
Only to give to such as have an incapacity.

Dean Goodluck

My faith I give to Roman Catholics ;
All my good works unto the Schismatics
Of Amsterdam ; my best civility
And courtship to an University ;
My modesty I give to soldiers bare ;
My patience let gamesters share :
Thou, Love, taught'st me, by making me
Love her that holds my love disparity,
Only to give to those that count my gifts indignity.

I give my reputation to those
Which were my friends ; mine industry to foes ;
To schoolmen I bequeath my doubtfulness ;
My sickness to physicians, or excess ;
To nature all that I in rhyme have writ ;
And to my company my wit :
Thou, Love, by making me adore
Her, who begot this love in me before,
Taught'st me to make, as though I gave,
    when I do but restore.

To him for whom the passing-bell next tolls,
I give my physic books ; my written rolls
Of moral counsels I to Bedlam give ;
My brazen medals unto them which live
In want of bread ; to them which pass among
All foreigners, mine English tongue :
Though, Love, by making me love one
Who thinks her friendship a fit portion
For younger lovers,
dost my gifts thus disproportion.

Therefore I'll give no more, but I'll undo
The world by dying, because love dies too.
Then all your beauties will be no more worth
Than gold in mines, where none doth draw it forth ;
And all your graces no more use shall have,
Than a sun-dial in a grave :
Thou, Love, taught'st me by making me
Love her who doth neglect both me and thee,
To invent, and practise this one way,
      to annihilate all three.

- The Will
by John Donne

Dean Goodluck

She Is Far From The Land

Thomas Moore

She is far from the land where her young hero sleeps,
And lovers are round her, sighing,
But coldly she turns from their gaze, and weeps,
For her heart in his grave is lying.

She sings the wild song of her dear native plains,
Every note which he loved awaking —
Ah! little they think, who delight in her strains,
How the heart of the Minstrel is breaking.

He had lived for his love, for his country he died,
They were all that to life had entwined him;
Nor soon shall the tears of his country be dried,
Nor long will his love stay behind him.

Poem in Art
She Is Far From The Land

Thomas Moore

She is far from the land where her young hero sleeps,
And lovers are round her, sighing;
But coldly she turns from their gaze, and weeps,
For her heart in his grave is lying.

She sings the wild song of her dear native plains,
Every note which he loved awaking; --
Ah! little they think, who delight in her strains,
How the heart of the Minstrel is breaking.

He had lived for his love, for his country he died,
They were all that to life had entwined him;
Nor soon shall the tears of his country be dried,
Nor long will his Love stay behind him.

- She Is Far From The Land
by Thomas Moore

Dean Goodluck

On Receiving Shell
A Curious Shell Verses
And A Copy Of Verses
From the Stunt Ladies

Poem
On Receiving A Curious Shell,
And A Copy Of Verses,
From the Same Ladies

John Keats

Hast thou from the caves of Golconda, a gem
Pure as the ice-drop that froze on the mountain?
Bright as the humming-bird's green diadem,
When it flutters in sun-beams
    that shine through a fountain?

Hast thou a goblet for dark sparkling wine?
That goblet right heavy, and massy, and gold?
And splendidly mark'd with the story divine
Of Armida the fair, and Rinaldo the bold?

Hast thou a steed with a mane richly flowing?
Hast thou a sword that thine enemy's smart is?
Hast thou a trumpet rich melodies blowing?
And wear'st thou the shield of the fam'd
Britomartis?

What is it that hangs from thy shoulder, so brave,
Embroidered with many a spring peering flower?
Is it a scarf that thy fair lady gave?
And hastest thou now to that fair lady's bower?

Dean Goodluck

Ah! courteous Sir Knight, with large joy
    thou art crown'd;
Full many the glories that brighten thy youth!
I will tell thee my blisses, which richly abound
In magical powers to bless, and to sooth.

On this scroll thou seest written in characters fair
A sun-beamy tale of a wreath, and a chain;
And, warrior, it nurtures the property rare
Of charming my mind from the trammels of pain.

This canopy mark: 'tis the work of a fay;
Beneath its rich shade did King Oberon languish,
When lovely Titania was far, far away,
And cruelly left him to sorrow, and anguish.

There, oft would he bring from his soft sighing lute
Wild strains to which, spell-bound,
    the nightingales listened;
The wondering spirits of heaven were mute,
And tears 'mong the dewdrops of morning
    oft glistened.

In this little dome, all those melodies strange,
Soft, plaintive, and melting, for ever will sigh;
Nor e'er will the notes from their tenderness change;
Nor e'er will the music of Oberon die.

So, when I am in a voluptuous vein,
I pillow my head on the sweets of the rose,
And list to the tale of the wreath, and the chain,
Till its echoes depart; then I sink to repose.

Adieu, valiant Eric! with joy thou art crown'd;
Full many the glories that brighten thy youth,
I too have my blisses, which richly abound
In magical powers, to bless and to sooth.

- On Receiving A Curious Shell,
And A Copy Of Verses,
From the Same Ladies
by John Keats

Dean Goodluck

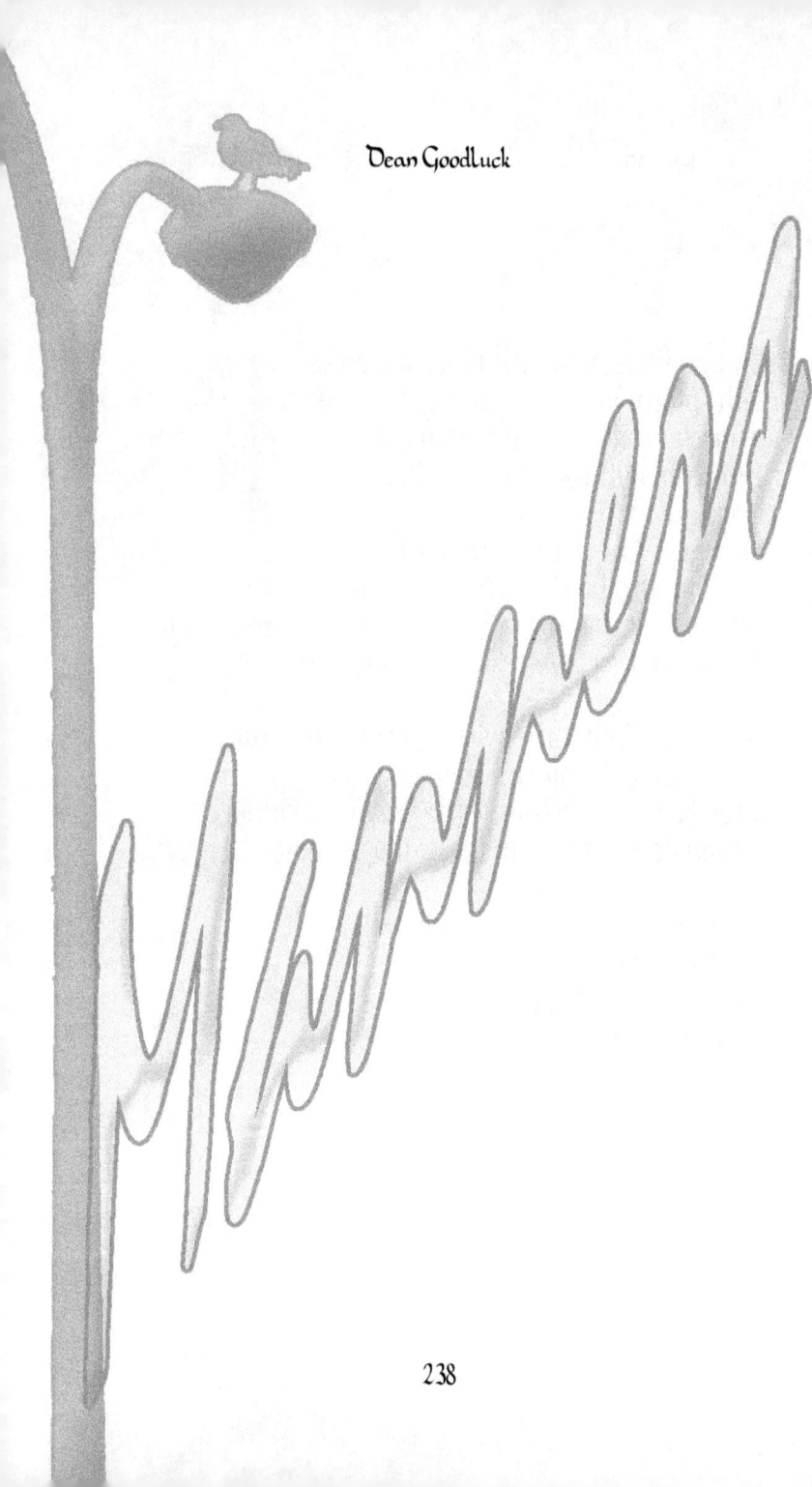

Manners

Poem
Manners
Ralph Waldo Emerson

Grace, Beauty, and Caprice
Build this golden portal;
Graceful women, chosen men,
Dazzle every mortal.
Their sweet and lofty countenance
His enchanted food;
He need not go to them, their forms
Beset his solitude.
He looketh seldom in their face,
His eyes explore the ground,--
The green grass is a looking-glass
Whereon their traits are found.
Little and less he says to them,
So dances his heart in his breast;
Their tranquil mien bereaveth him
Of wit, of words, of rest.
Too weak to win, too fond to shun
The tyrants of his doom,
The much deceived Endymion
Slips behind a tomb.

- Manners
by Ralph Waldo Emerson

Dean Goodluck

When Far-Spent Night

Poem
When Far-Spent Night
Sir Philip Sidney

When far-spent night persuades each mortal eye,
To whom nor art nor nature granted light,
To lay his then mark-wanting shafts of sight,
Clos'd with their quivers, in sleep's armory;

With windows ope then most my mind doth lie,
Viewing the shape of darkness and delight,
Takes in that sad hue which the inward night
Of his maz'd powers keeps perfect harmony;

But when birds charm, and that sweet air which is
Morn's messenger, with rose enamel'd skies,
Calls each wight to salute the flower of bliss,

In tomb of lids then buried are mine eyes,
Forc'd by their lord, who is asham'd to find
Such light in sense, with such a darken'd mind.

- When Far-Spent Night
by Sir Philip Sidney

Dean Goodluck

Paradise Lost

Poem
Paradise Lost: Book 01
(lines 655-798)

John Milton

Thither, if but to pry, shall be perhaps
Our first eruption--thither, or elsewhere;
For this infernal pit shall never hold
Celestial Spirits in bondage, nor th' Abyss
Long under darkness cover. But these thoughts
Full counsel must mature. Peace is despaired;
For who can think submission? War, then, war
Open or understood, must be resolved."
He spake; and, to confirm his words, outflew
Millions of flaming swords, drawn from the thighs
Of mighty Cherubim; the sudden blaze
Far round illumined Hell. Highly they raged
Against the Highest, and fierce with grasped arms
Clashed on their sounding shields the din of war,
Hurling defiance toward the vault of Heaven.
There stood a hill not far, whose grisly top
Belched fire and rolling smoke; the rest entire
Shone with a glossy scurf--undoubted sign
That in his womb was hid metallic ore,

Dean Goodluck

The work of sulphur. Thither, winged with speed,
A numerous brigade hastened: as when bands
Of pioneers, with spade and pickaxe armed,
Forerun the royal camp, to trench a field,
Or cast a rampart. Mammon led them on--
Mammon, the least erected Spirit that fell
From Heaven; for even in Heaven
    his looks and thoughts
Were always downward bent, admiring more
The riches of heaven's pavement, trodden gold,
Than aught divine or holy else enjoyed
In vision beatific. By him first
Men also, and by his suggestion taught,
Ransacked the centre, and with impious hands
Rifled the bowels of their mother Earth
For treasures better hid. Soon had his crew
Opened into the hill a spacious wound,
And digged out ribs of gold. Let none admire
That riches grow in Hell; that soil may best
Deserve the precious bane. And here let those
Who boast in mortal things, and wondering tell
Of Babel, and the works of Memphian kings,
Learn how their greatest monuments of fame
And strength, and art, are easily outdone

By Spirits reprobate, and in an hour
What in an age they, with incessant toil
And hands innumerable, scarce perform.
Nigh on the plain, in many cells prepared,
That underneath had veins of liquid fire
Sluiced from the lake, a second multitude
With wondrous art founded the massy ore,
Severing each kind, and scummed the bullion-dross.
A third as soon had formed within the ground
A various mould, and from the boiling cells
By strange conveyance filled each hollow nook;
As in an organ, from one blast of wind,
To many a row of pipes the sound-board breathes.
Anon out of the earth a fabric huge
Rose like an exhalation, with the sound
Of dulcet symphonies and voices sweet--
Built like a temple, where pilasters round
Were set, and Doric pillars overlaid
With golden architrave; nor did there want
Cornice or frieze, with bossy sculptures graven;
The roof was fretted gold. Not Babylon
Nor great Alcairo such magnificence
Equalled in all their glories, to enshrine
Belus or Serapis their gods, or seat

Dean Goodluck

Their kings, when Egypt with Assyria strove
In wealth and luxury. Th' ascending pile
Stood fixed her stately height, and straight the doors,
Opening their brazen folds, discover, wide
Within, her ample spaces o'er the smooth
And level pavement: from the arched roof,
Pendent by subtle magic, many a row
Of starry lamps and blazing cressets, fed
With naptha and asphaltus, yielded light
As from a sky. The hasty multitude
Admiring entered; and the work some praise,
And some the architect. His hand was known
In Heaven by many a towered structure high,
Where sceptred Angels held their residence,
And sat as Princes, whom the supreme King
Exalted to such power, and gave to rule,
Each in his Hierarchy, the Orders bright.
Nor was his name unheard or unadored
In ancient Greece; and in Ausonian land
Men called him Mulciber; and how he fell
From Heaven they fabled, thrown by angry Jove
Sheer o'er the crystal battlements: from morn
To noon he fell, from noon to dewy eve,

A summer's day, and with the setting sun
Dropt from the zenith, like a falling star,
On Lemnos, th' Aegaean isle. Thus they relate,
Erring; for he with this rebellious rout
Fell long before; nor aught aviled him now
To have built in Heaven high towers;
    nor did he scape
By all his engines, but was headlong sent,
With his industrious crew, to build in Hell.
Meanwhile the winged Heralds, by command
Of sovereign power, with awful ceremony
And trumpet's sound, throughout the host proclaim
A solemn council forthwith to be held
At Pandemonium, the high capital
Of Satan and his peers. Their summons called
From every band and squared regiment
By place or choice the worthiest: they anon
With hundreds and with thousands trooping came
Attended. All access was thronged; the gates
And porches wide, but chief the spacious hall
(Though like a covered field, where champions bold
Wont ride in armed, and at the Soldan's chair
Defied the best of Paynim chivalry

Dean Goodluck

To mortal combat, or career with lance),
Thick swarmed, both on the ground and in the air,
Brushed with the hiss of rustling wings. As bees
In spring-time, when the Sun with Taurus rides.
Pour forth their populous youth about the hive
In clusters; they among fresh dews and flowers
Fly to and fro, or on the smoothed plank,
The suburb of their straw-built citadel,
New rubbed with balm, expatiate, and confer
Their state-affairs: so thick the airy crowd
Swarmed and were straitened; till, the signal given,
Behold a wonder! They but now who seemed
In bigness to surpass Earth's giant sons,
Now less than smallest dwarfs, in narrow room
Throng numberless--like that pygmean race
Beyond the Indian mount; or faery elves,
Whose midnight revels, by a forest-side
Or fountain, some belated peasant sees,
Or dreams he sees, while overhead the Moon
Sits arbitress, and nearer to the Earth
Wheels her pale course:
        they, on their mirth and dance
Intent, with jocund music charm his ear;

At once with joy and fear his heart rebounds.
Thus incorporeal Spirits to smallest forms
Reduced their shapes immense, and were at large,
Though without number still, amidst the hall
Of that infernal court. But far within,
And in their own dimensions like themselves,
The great Seraphic Lords and Cherubim
In close recess and secret conclave sat,
A thousand demi-gods on golden seats,
Frequent and full. After short silence then,
And summons read, the great consult began.

- from Paradise Lost: Book 01 (lines 655-798)
by John Milton

Dean Goodluck

O Captain! my Captain!

O Captain! my Captain!
Rise up and hear the bells;
Rise up—for you the flag is flung—
for you the bugle trills;
For you bouquets and ribbon'd wreaths—
for you the shores a-crowding;
For you they call, the swaying mass,
their eager faces turning;
Here Captain! dear father!
This arm beneath your head;
It is some dream that on the deck,
You've fallen cold and dead.

Walt Whitman

Poem in Art
O Captain! My Captain!
- Walt Whitman

O Captain! my Captain! rise up and hear the bells;
Rise up--for you the flag is flung--
　　for you the bugle trills;
For you bouquets and ribbon'd wreaths--
　　for you the shores a-crowding;
For you they call, the swaying mass,
　　their eager faces turning;
Here Captain! dear father!
This arm beneath your head;
It is some dream that on the deck,
You've fallen cold and dead.

- from O Captain! My Captain!
by Walt Whitman

Publisher's Blog:
WcP Blog | World Culture Pictorial
www.worldculturepictorial.com

"Great culture sharing.
This is really important to show
all over the world and different cultures
and nature to whole world."
- Anonymous

"I always take pleasure in your articles.
You have a gift for discussing such
stirring topics in ingenious yet amusing ways.
Your posts help us realize that our troubles are
typical, and we can solve them
in ready to lend a hand ways..."
- Angela

"So poetic..."
- Anonymous

Dean Goodluck

Other Volumes in the Series

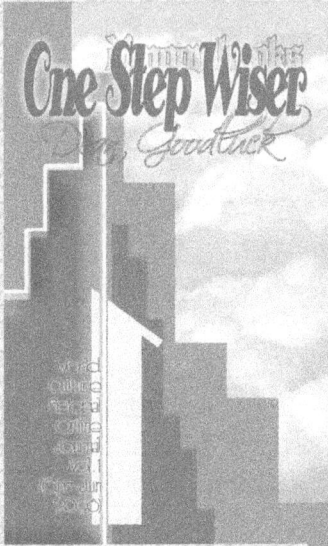

One Step Wiser

Two Steps Wiser

full color print
through and through
including art images

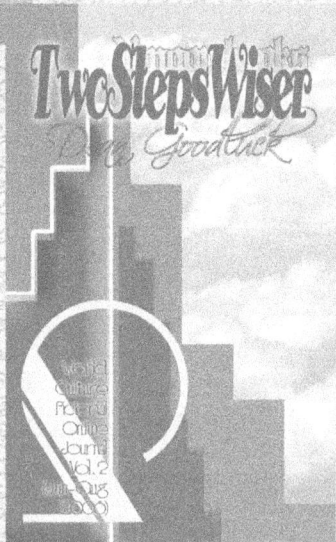

www.worldculturepictorial.com/one-step-wiser.html

Other Volumes in the Series

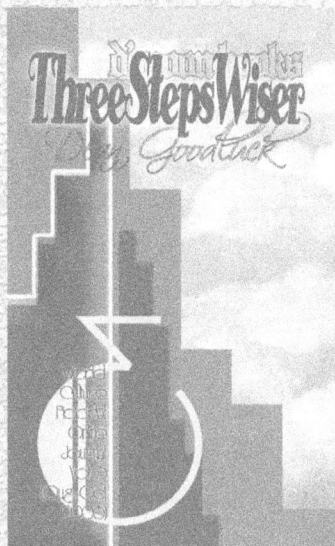

full color print
through and through
including art images

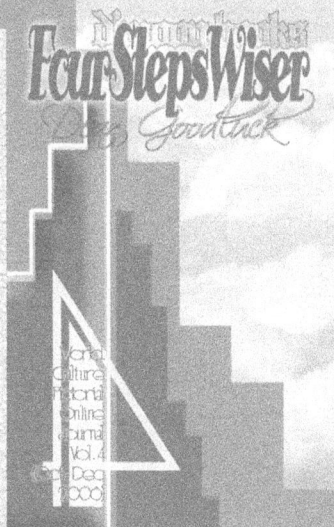

www.worldculturepictorial.com/one-step-wiser.html

Dean Goodluck

Other Volumes in the Series

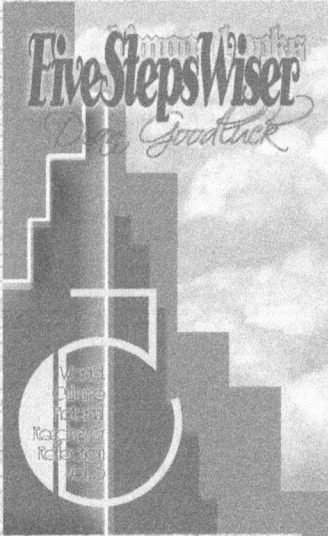

b&w interior print
on classic creme paper
including art images

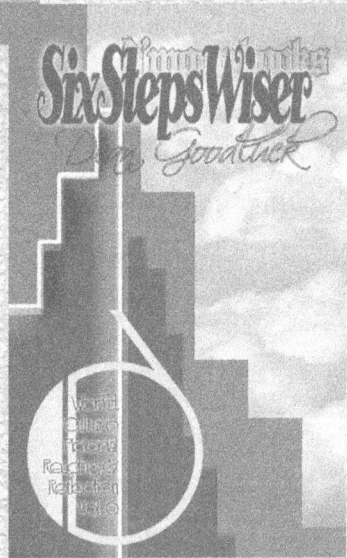

www.worldculturepictorial.com/one-step-wiser.html

www.ingramcontent.com/pod-product-compliance
Lightning Source LLC
Chambersburg PA
CBHW022048020426
42335CB00012B/593